THE BEST OF
Personal Excellence

The Magazine of Life Enrichment   **Volume 1**

This compilation:
© **1998 by Executive Excellence Publishing**
Each article is copyrighted separately by the authors.

All Rights Reserved. No portion of this book may be reproduced or transmitted in any form or by any means, electronic or mechanical, including photocopying, recording, or by any information storage and retrieval system, without written permission from the publisher, except for brief quotations used in critical and certain other noncommercial uses permitted by copyright law. For permission requests, please write to:

Executive Excellence Publishing
1344 East 1120 South
Provo, Utah 84606
phone: (801) 375-5960
fax: (801) 377-5960
e-mail: execexcl@itsnet.com
web: http:\\www.eep.com

Ordering Information:
Individual Sales: Executive Excellence Publishing products are available through most bookstores. They also can be ordered directly from Executive Excellence at the address above.

Quantity Sales: Executive Excellence Publishing products are available at special quantity discounts when purchased in bulk by corporations, associations, libraries, and others, or for college textbook/course adoptions. Please write to the address above or call Executive Excellence Publishing Book Sales Division at 1-800-304-9782.

Orders for U.S. and Canadian trade bookstores and wholesalers: Executive Excellence Publishing books and audio tapes are available to the trade through LPC Group/Login Trade. Please contact LPC at 1436 West Randolph Street, Chicago, IL 60607, or call 1-800-626-4330.

First edition: January 1998
Printed in the United States of America
10 9 8 7 6 5 4 3 2 1   02 01 00 99 98 97

ISBN: 1-890009-01-6

Also available on audio (two sets):
ISBN 1-890009-00-8 volume 1
ISBN 1-890009-28-8 volume 2

Cover design by Joe McGovern
Printed by Publishers Press

CONTENTS

Introduction 7

SECTION 1. *Preparation* 9

1. *In Pursuit of Excellence*
   by Michael Jordan 11

2. *Quality of Life*
   by Stephen R. Covey 15

3. *Be Positive*
   by Ruth Stafford Peale 19

4. *Smart Talk*
   by Lou Tice 21

5. *Why Be and Do Good?*
   by Harold Kushner 27

6. *Winner's Edge*
   by Denis Waitley 29

7. *Get Ego Out of the Way*
   by Monica L. Simons 33

8. *The Puzzle of Personal Excellence*
   by Dianne Booher 37

9. *How to Get What You Want Out of Life*
   by Dr. Joyce Brothers 43

10. *The Winner's Attitude*
    by Vince Lombardi 45

SECTION 2. *Performance* 49

11. *Four Principles*
    by Steve Young 51

12. *Olympic Dreams*
    by Les Brown 55

13. *Creating Affluence*
    by Deepak Chopra 57

14. *Quest for Freedom*
    by Pope John Paul II 59

15. *You Can Do It!*
    by Mary Kay Ash 63

16. *Never Surrender Leadership*
    by Robert H. Schuller 65

17. *Ten Natural Laws*
    by Hyrum W. Smith...69

18. *Work Leads to Success*
    by Harvey Mackay 73

19. *The Cycle of Success*
    by Roger Staubach...75

20. *Going the Distance*
    by George Sheehan 77

21. *What Makes for Success?*
    by Dave Thomas 81

22. *Struggle for Balance*
    by Ken Blanchard 85

23. *Maximum Achievement*
    by Brian Tracy 87

SECTION 3. *Recovery* 91

24. *Bouncing Back*
    by Wally Amos...93

25. *Women at Work*
    by Judy Woodruff 99

26. *The Bane of Busyness*
    by Eileen McDargh 101

27. *Balanced Success*
    by Zig Ziglar 103

28. *Make the Connection*
    by Oprah Winfrey 107

29. *The Maturity Challenge*
    by Leo Buscaglia 111

30. *Without Clothes, We're All Naked*
    by Carla Perez 115

31. *From Panic to Power*
    by Lucinda Bassett...117

32. *Power to Recover*
    by Betty Ford 121

SECTION 4. *Life Values* 125

33. *Life Values*
    by William Bennett 127

34. *A Call to Action*
    by Hillary Rodham Clinton 129

35. *The Joy of Service*
   by Arnold Schwarzenegger.......................................131

36. *Lessons in Life*
   by Barbara Bush 133

37. *Values Make Us Stronger*
   by Dan Quayle and Diane Medved 135

38. *Faith in Action*
   by Lady Margaret Thatcher......................................139

39. *Challenge of Change*
   by Rosalynn Carter 141

40. *Three Words*
   by Martha Saunders..143

41. *My Pyramid of Success*
   by John Wooden 145

42. *Cynicism or Faith?*
   by Al Gore...149

SECTION 5. *Ongoing Growth* 153

43. *The Art of Self-Motivation*
   by Bonnie St. John Deane 155

44. *A Responsible Life*
   by Nathaniel Branden 159

45. *Mr. Peak Performance*
   an interview with Charles Garfield 163

46. *The Taming of the Ego*
   by Wayne Dyer 167

47. *Power in the Positive*
   by Norman Vincent Peale 171

48. *Giving and Receiving Criticism*
   by Patti Hathaway...175

49. *Courage to Change*
   by Sheila Murray Bethel..179

50. *The Power of Forgiveness*
   by John Gray 181

51. *Everybody's Doing It? That's No Excuse!*
   by Laura Schlessinger..185

52. *The Emancipation Proclamation*
   by Ken Shelton..187

Introduction

This book features some of the most popular articles to appear in the first two years of *Personal Excellence* magazine (1996-97).

One Purpose

Our initial intent—to provide a whole-life, values-based digest of the best thinking on personal, family, and professional development—is reflected in both the structure and content of this book.

Five Sections

Please notice that we have organized material into five sections. The first section focuses on foundations or preparations needed for success. The second section highlights on-the-field performance, the payoff of preparation. The third section suggests ways to recover from setbacks, bounce back, and achieve balanced success. The fourth section concentrates on life values, beliefs and principles. And the last section points to on-going growth, learning, and development.

No Corner on Truth

We at Executive Excellence Publishing respect the fact that truth and light can be found in every race, place, religion, culture, and society. We keep an open mind and an open editorial policy. No one consultant, professor, leader, priest, or professional has a corner on truth and enlightenment.

Excellence in Action™

My hope is that these articles help you discover what you need to be and do to reach your own personal excellence. I encourage you to create your own *Excellence in Action* agenda, based on the ideas in this book and your own promptings.

Ken Shelton
Editor of *Personal Excellence*

SECTION 1

Preparation

1

In Pursuit of Excellence

by Michael Jordan

I *have the goal* of being the best, but I approach everything step by step using short-term goals. When I meet one goal, I set another reasonable goal I can achieve if I work hard. Each success leads to the next one. Each time I visualize where I want to be and what kind of person and player I want to become. I approach it with the end in mind. I know exactly where I want to go, and I focus on getting there. As I reach those goals, I gain a little more confidence. It's all mental for me. I never write anything down. I just concentrate on the next step.

I'm not afraid to ask anybody anything. Why should I be afraid? My attitude is: "Help me; give me direction."

I could apply that approach to anything I might do. It's no different for the person whose goal is to become a doctor. All those steps are like pieces of a puzzle. They all come together to form a picture. If it's complete, you reach your goal. If not, don't get down on yourself.

Don't Think About Failure

I never look at the consequences of failing, because when you think about the consequences, you always think of a negative result. If I'm jumping into any situation, I'm thinking I'm going to be successful—not about what happens if I fail.

Some people get frozen by fear of failure by thinking about the possibility of a negative result. They might be afraid of looking bad or being embarrassed. I realized that if I was going to achieve anything in life, I had to be aggressive. I had to get out there and go for it. I don't believe you can achieve anything by being passive.

I know fear is an obstacle for some people, but to me it's an illusion. Any fear is an illusion. You think something is standing in your way, but nothing is there—only an opportunity to do your best and gain some success.

If it turns out my best isn't good enough, then at least I'll never be able to look back and say I was too afraid to try. Maybe I just didn't have it. Maybe I just wasn't good enough. There's nothing wrong with that and nothing to be afraid of either. Failure always made me try harder the next time.

My advice is, "Think positive, and find fuel in failure." Sometimes failure gets you closer to where you want to be. The greatest inventions in the world had hundreds of failures before answers were found.

Fear sometimes comes from a lack of focus or concentration. If you know you are doing the right things, just relax and perform. Forget about the outcome. You can't control anything anyway.

When you make a presentation in business, you may do all the things necessary, but then it's out of your hands. Either the clients like the presentation, or they don't. It's up to the client or the buyer. So don't worry about it.

I can accept failure. Everyone fails at something. But I can't accept not trying. It doesn't matter if you win as long as you give everything in your heart and work at it 110 percent. If you put in the work, the results will come. I can't do things halfheartedly, because I know if I do, then I can expect halfhearted results. That's why I approach practices the same way I approach games. I can't dog it during practice and then, when I need that extra push late in the game, expect it to be there.

But that's how a lot of people approach things. And that's why they fail. They sound like they're committed to being the best they can be. They say all the right things, make all the proper appearances. But they're looking for reasons instead of answers.

Overcome Obstacles

You see it all the time in business. There are a million excuses for not paying the price: "If only I was given a particular opportunity," "If only the boss liked me better, I could accomplish this or that." Nothing but excuses.

That's not to say there aren't obstacles or distractions. If you're trying to achieve, there will be roadblocks. But obstacles don't have to stop you. If you run into a wall, don't give up. Figure out how to climb it, go through it, or work around it.

You have to stick to your plan. A lot of people try to pull you down to their level because they can't achieve certain things. But very few people get anywhere by taking shortcuts. More people gain success the honest way, by setting their goals and committing themselves to achieving those goals.

Our society tends to glamorize individual success without considering the entire process. What if you have a CEO with a great idea, but he doesn't have the people to make it happen? If you don't have all the pieces in place, particularly at the front lines, that idea doesn't mean a thing. You can have the greatest salespeople in the world, but if the people making the product aren't any good, no one will buy it.

Managers, like coaches, have to find ways to utilize individual talents in the best interests of the company. It's a selfless process. In our society sometimes it's hard to come to grips with filling a role instead of trying to be a superstar. We tend to ignore or fail to respect all the parts that make the whole possible. Talent wins games, but teamwork and intelligence win championships.

Everything I achieved can be traced back to the way I approached and applied the fundamentals, the basic building blocks or principles that make everything work. I don't care what you're doing—you can't skip fundamentals if you want to be the best. But some guys don't want to deal with that. They're looking for instant gratification, so maybe they skip a few steps. They're so focused on composing a masterpiece that they never master the scales. You can get away with it through the early stages, but it's going to catch up with you eventually. The minute you get away from fundamentals—whether it's proper technique, work ethic, or mental preparation—the bottom can fall out of your game, your schoolwork, your job, whatever you're doing.

When you understand the building blocks, you see how the entire operation works. And that allows you to operate more intelligently. It sounds easy, but it isn't. You have to monitor your fundamentals constantly because the only thing that changes will be your attention to them. The fundamentals will never change. There is a right way and a wrong way to do things. Get the fundamentals down, and the level of everything you do will rise.

Lead by Example

I've always tried to lead by example. I never tried to motivate by talking because I don't think words ever mean as much as action. A picture carries a thousand words. So I tried to paint a picture of hard work and discipline. Why not? If the person out front doesn't work hard, why should anyone else?

A leader has to earn that title. You aren't the leader just because you're the best player on the team, the smartest person in the class, or the most popular. No one can give you that title either. You have to gain the respect of those around you by your actions. You have to be consistent in your approach, whether it's basketball practice, a sales meeting, or dealing with your family. Those around you have to know what to expect. They have to be confident that you'll be there, that your performance will be consistent from game to game, particularly when things get tight.

Ultimately, coaches or players can say anything they want, but if they don't back it up with performance and hard work, the talking doesn't mean a thing. A leader can't make any excuses. There has to be quality in everything you do—off the court, on the court, in the classroom, on the playground, inside the meeting room, outside of work. You have to transfer those skills, that drive, to whatever environment you're in. And you have to be willing to sacrifice certain individual goals, if necessary, for the good of the team. A leader is also a person who has had past successes in certain situations and isn't afraid of taking the chance to lead others down that road again.

Along the way, you also have to stand up for what you believe and hold on to your convictions. Every home, every business, and every neighborhood needs someone to lead.

Michael Jordan is the author of *I Can't Accept Not Trying* (Harper San Francisco) and plays basketball for the Chicago Bulls. This article is adapted from his book and is used with permission.

2

Quality of Life

by Stephen R. Covey

In recent years, I have met thousands of people who want to improve the quality of their lives, often as a way of finding more meaning, happiness, and fulfillment.

Most people possess far more capability, creativity, talent, initiative, and resourcefulness than their present jobs allow or require them to use.

Sadly, I see many people trying to open the door to quality of life using the wrong keys—using ill-advised approaches and shortcut, manipulative practices learned in academic, athletic, social, and business systems.

The key to quality of life is the quality of your relationships. When you apply manipulative practices to your personal relationships, the "farms" of your life, you fail to harvest the fruit you desire. The principles of agriculture apply equally to human culture.

Motive and Means Do Matter

Some people justify heavy-handed means in the name of virtuous ends. They say that "ethics" and "principles" sometimes have to take a back seat to expediency and profits. Many people see no correlation between the quality of their personal lives at home and the quality of their products and services at work. Because of the social and political environment in their organizations and the fragmented market outside, they can abuse relationships at will and still get short-term results.

Our heroes are often people who make a lot of money. And when some hero—an actor, entertainer, athlete, or other professional—suggests that we can get what we want by practicing hardball negotiation, closing win-lose deals, and playing by our own rules, then we listen to them, especially if social norms reinforce what they say.

I see people trying to do it all over a weekend—trying to rebuild their marriage over a weekend, trying to change a company culture over a weekend, trying to lose weight over a weekend. Some things just can't be done over a weekend.

In school, we ask students to tell us what we told them; we test them on our lectures. They figure out the system, party and procrastinate, then cram and feed it back to us to get the grades. They think all of life operates on the same shortcut system.

But the quick, easy, free, and fun approach won't work on "the farm" because there we're subject to natural laws and governing principles. Natural laws, based upon principles, operate regardless of our awareness of them or our obedience to them.

Often habits of ineffectiveness are rooted in our social conditioning toward quick-fix, short-term thinking. In life, as in school, many of us procrastinate and then cram. But does cramming work on a farm? Can you go two weeks without milking the cow, and then get out there and milk like crazy?

We might laugh at such ludicrous approaches in agriculture, but then employ them in corporate cultures.

The only thing that endures over time is the law of the farm: I must prepare the ground, put the seed in, cultivate it, weed it, water it, then gradually nurture growth and development to full maturity. So also in a marriage, or in helping a teenager through a difficult identity crisis—there is no quick fix.

Center on Timeless Principles

Correct principles are like compasses: They are always pointing the way. And if we know how to read them, we won't get lost, confused, or fooled by conflicting voices and values.

Principles are not invented by us or by society: They are the laws of the universe that pertain to human relationships and human organizations. They are part of the human condition, consciousness, and conscience. To the degree people recognize and live in harmony with such basic principles as fairness, equity, justice, integrity, honesty, and trust, they progress.

Moreover, people instinctively trust those whose character and competence are founded upon correct principles, because trust is related to one's trustworthiness over time.

Most people prefer to work on their appearance or personality, not on their character. The former may involve learning a new skill or style or image, but the latter involves changing habits, developing virtues, disciplining appetites and passions, keeping promises, and being considerate of the feelings and convictions of others. Character development is the true test and manifestation of our maturity. To value oneself and yet subordinate oneself to higher purposes and principles is the essence of highest humanity and the foundation of effective leadership.

Principle-centered leaders are men and women of character who work with competence "on farms" with "seed and soil" and who work in harmony with natural, "true north" principles and with the law of the harvest. They build those principles into the center of their lives, into the center of their relationships and their mission statements.

Positive personality traits, while often essential for success, constitute secondary greatness. To focus on personality before character is to try to grow the tree without the roots.

If we consistently use personality techniques and skills to enhance our social interactions, we may truncate the vital character base. We simply can't have the fruits without the roots. Private victory precedes public victory. Self-mastery and self-discipline are the character roots of good relationships with others.

If we use human influence strategies and tactics to get other people to do what we want, we may succeed short term; but over time, our duplicity and insincerity will breed distrust. Everything we do will be perceived as manipulative. We may have the "right" rhetoric, style, and even intention, but without trust, we won't achieve primary greatness.

In a social or academic system, you may make favorable first impressions through charm; you may win through intimidation. But secondary personality traits alone have little worth in long-term relationships. True motives eventually surface.

Many people with secondary greatness—social status, position, fame, wealth, or talent—lack primary greatness or goodness of character. And this void is evident in every long-term relationship they have, whether it is with a business associate, a spouse, a friend, or a teenage child. It is character that communicates most eloquently.

The place to begin building any relationship is inside ourselves, inside our circles of influence, our own characters. As we become independent—proactive, centered in correct principles, value-driven and able to organize and execute around the priorities in our lives with integrity—we then can choose to become interdependent: capable of building rich, enduring relationships.

Three Character Traits

Three character traits are essential to primary greatness:

• *Integrity.* As we clearly identify our values and proactively organize and execute around our priorities, we develop self-awareness and self-value by making and keeping meaningful promises and commitments. If we can't make and keep commitments, our word becomes meaningless.

• *Maturity.* If a person can express his or her feelings and convictions with courage balanced with consideration for the feelings and convictions of another person, he or she is mature. If the person lacks internal maturity and emotional strength, he or she might try to borrow strength from position, power, credentials, seniority, or affiliations.

• *Abundance Mentality.* The abundance mentality—the idea that there is plenty out there for everybody—flows out of a deep sense of personal worth and security. It results in sharing recognition, profits, and responsibility. It opens up creative new options and alternatives. It turns personal joy and fulfillment outward. It recognizes unlimited possibilities for positive interaction, growth, and development.

As we give grace to others, we receive more grace ourselves. As we affirm people and believe in their capacity to grow, as we bless them even when they are cursing or judging us—we build primary greatness into our personality and character.

Stephen R. Covey, the author of *The 7 Habits of Highly Effective People* and *Principle-Centered Leadership* and co-author of *First Things First,* is the co-chairman of FrankilnCovey Co.

3

Be Positive

by Ruth Stafford Peale

Since my husband, Norman Vincent Peale, passed away, I have a new career. At the age of 90, I'm managing the Peale Center and speaking more to groups of people. My message is simple: If you have a positive mind and faith, instead of being discouraged when something bad happens, you will learn lessons that will be for your good, and you will grow from the experience.

So many people are negative thinkers, simply because they get discouraged. They want results fast and easy. Life isn't like that. Norman and I struggled for six years during the Depression to build the church in New York. He became very discouraged. In 1938 we went to England for a summer vacation. Norman was so discouraged that he could not say anything positive. I remember sitting with him on a bench in the garden of the hotel. I got tired of hearing him complain. So I said, "Now look, Norman. You talk about positive thinking, and yet all you're doing is thinking negatively. I think what you need to do is to practice what you preach about faith and positive thinking." I guess I was forceful enough that finally he got up and said, "Boy, I'm all enthused again. Let's go home right away." I said, "No, we're going to finish our vacation."

As Norman started to practice positive thinking, he considered new ways to do the work. For example, he said, "If they're not going to come here to hear me, I'll go out." So he accepted any invitation to speak that came along. Well, things began to pick up. He went on the radio, and that helped to bring people into the church. And finally when the church was packed and full of people, it remained that way until 1984 when he retired.

A person needs the power of positive thinking to experience the best in life and to enjoy the spiritual dimension. You see, positive thinking is just another way of talking about faith—the belief that God is always there to help direct your life, and to help you find happiness and fulfillment in your work and your relationships, including marriage and family. Positive thinking is even more important today because many people are discouraged, if not downright depressed. They feel lonely and isolated. They're also under great stress because they've never learned how to control their emotions. When your mind is full of fear, doubt, and clutter, good ideas can't get through. You get your best ideas and make your best decisions when you're relaxed, open to impressions, and responsive to them.

Also, if you want to lead the good life, you need to be a good person. Many people are confused because they see "bad" people who have very good lives—full of comforts and conveniences. But, you see, to me that is a superficial expression of the good life. The good life is one in which you are at peace in your inner soul. When you are at peace with yourself and others, and when you have good habits of positive thinking and living, you can make each day a better day.

You must do many things on your own, exercising your creativity, judgment, initiative, and resourcefulness. You also need a clear idea of who you are and what you can do.

When success comes to you, it may have a strange emptiness to it, if others have not been part of your life or if you have not experienced the spiritual dimension of life.

Ruth Stafford Peale is author of *Secrets of Staying in Love* and chairman of the Peale Center for Christian Living.

4

Smart Talk

by Lou Tice

How do you get from where you are now—from here, this present moment—to there, where you want to go? What is the process? I see five steps.

1. First, you've got to figure out the "there." The there may be a new marriage, a new family, business expansion, a new home, increasing your income, or improving your health.

I encourage you to think in ideals. Think in ideals even when all about you is insanity and denial. An ideal is an image, vision, fantasy, dream, or aspiration that exists only in the mind. You simply look at current reality, the way things actually are now, and then you say to yourself, "What would be ideal? What would be the ideal way to treat my spouse and children? What would be the ideal career for me? What would be the ideal month, week, day?"

You've got to know what you want. Start with the end result. Creating an ideal, goal, or vision is just making constructive use of your imagination. You construct a future in your mind before it ever occurs. Don't get trapped by your present reality—what you have or how effective you are at the moment. People who are immersed in a present reality often think they "know the truth" about it. But they don't.

Make sure your reasons (motives) are right. Why do you want it? How unselfish is your motive? What drives you? You don't need to compete with other people. You don't have to be the best in your profession. You set your own ideals. What matters is making the world around you a better place by creating happiness-producing events for yourself and other people. You make it happen because it's the right thing to do. You do it with the right spirit of intent. You give with no ulterior motive. You work out of a sense of purpose in your life, and the purposes and the reasons just keep getting bigger and deeper.

2. Engage in constructive self-talk. Constructive self-talk is what I call smart talk. Self-talk is the continual dialogue you have with yourself. It is also the raw material from which you manufacture your own self-image. Your subconscious believes what you tell yourself and then makes sure you act according to your beliefs. Language has power over behavior. If you control your self-talk, you can use your subconscious to help you achieve your goals. You move toward, and become like, that which you think about. Your present thoughts determine your future. What you repeatedly tell yourself with your own self-talk determines your beliefs and self-image, which affects your behavior. Unless you change your stored beliefs by changing your self-talk, you won't alter your behavior. Your future will look a lot like your past.

I encourage you to review and relive your successes. You need to feel good about yourself to get from here to there. You need to feel that your life matters. You need to feel happy with yourself and find increasing joy in your daily work as you achieve what you want to achieve. Your progress will accelerate when you take time to reflect upon your success. I'm convinced that we pass too lightly upon our successes. We tend to say, "Oh, it was nothing" or "I was just lucky." And by saying that, we convince ourselves that we had little to do with it.

To reinforce your success, you might write a list of 10 of your most prominent achievements and reflect on this list for a moment each day. By doing this, you greatly enhance your ability to replicate your success and build on your past accomplishments.

3. Use your creative imagination to set and imprint goals. One way to use your forethought—your ability to think ahead— is to set goals. Goal setting is a deliberate attempt to define the quality standards that will guide you into the future. You must have a target, a picture of what you want. If you don't give yourself a goal for the future, you'll recreate the one you've got. So tomorrow won't look any different than today.

Goal setting is deliberately giving yourself a new idea of how things will be in the future. How do you want things to look? If you don't give yourself that ideal, you'll make the next year, the next generation, or the next situation look like the last one. Goal setting, done correctly, causes growth and development. Goal setting is changing where you belong in your mind. It's expanding the limits, expanding the environment, developing new standards to release your inhibitive, restrictive behavior. Goal setting is establishing a new significance. The process of setting goals increases your awareness to information and resources in your environment that will help you achieve the desired outcome or goal.

When you clearly set a goal for yourself, you're declaring that some things are more significant than others. You're defining what's important to you. Until then, resources and information that would help you achieve the goal could be right in front of you, but you won't see them. You'll block them out. Goal setting allows more essential information to get through.

Don't limit your aspirations, goals, and dreams based upon the resources available to you now. These resources may be all around you, without your knowing it, because they're not important at the moment. But as soon as you declare them significant, suddenly they appear. You think you're lucky or that it's coincidence. So the goal comes first, then you perceive.

4. Start taking action, and use feedback to correct course. Don't wait for the big time—the big time is where you are at the moment. You don't wait until you develop before you take action. You take action on the level you're living presently. Or you will never take action. You do things at whatever level, at whatever place—your work, your community, your family. You've got to turn and face it now.

Just start where you are. Don't wait until you're good and ready before you take action. Take action now because you'll get better as you go. If I had waited until I was as good as I am now to start, I never would have started. I was as good as I could be when I started, but I got better every day.

Get feedback and make adjustments. We are teleological in nature. We have the ability to seek out objects. A teleological mechanism might operate on sound, like sonar; or on electronic waves, like radar; or on metallic attraction, like a magnet. A teleological mechanism can change directions after it's released. It doesn't care where it starts; it only cares where it is now in relation to where it intends to be. A teleological mechanism also has a feedback system. If you trigger the heat-seeking missile, as it goes toward the heat of the jet, it won't go in a straight line. It moves around. It says to itself, "Where am I, where am I, where am I?" And the question is "Where am I in relation to what?" And the answer is "Where am I in relation to where I want to go?"

We move toward pictures; we move toward ideas; we move toward the image that we hold in our minds. So we say, "I've got an idea of what I want to create." We need the idea. Your scanning and guidance mechanism is your sensory feedback. But keeping on track is not easy because getting and accepting accurate, truthful feedback is not easy. But you need this feedback to progress, to move toward the target. Your senses are constantly scanning the environment for information to tell you how you are doing in relation to your target goals.

If you deny the feedback, you'll find that you can't go very fast. You need feedback from other people and your own senses to correct as you proceed toward the target. As a missile pursues the target, the heat of the jet, it says, How am I doing? This teleological mechanism knows when it's off the beam.

When you're someplace where you don't know anybody, or when you're in a new position or a new job, or when you're making changes, or when change is thrust upon you, you say to yourself, "My gosh, this can't be right, or I wouldn't feel this bad." This increases the likelihood of failure, and your subconscious says, "Don't be stupid. Stay where you're already good. Stay with what and who you know. Stay in your own neighborhood." We start to create reasons why we shouldn't go to the next plateau or level. We misinterpret "negative" feedback, thinking "negative" is bad. Negative just means avoidant. It means to move back or retreat. Positive does not mean good. Positive just means to move toward, to seek out.

The beam for you is the image of what you're trying to create. When you're on the beam, you're in your comfort zone. You don't get much comfort-zone feedback. But when you're off the beam (for you), you'll get hit with anxiety or tension. You interpret this feedback as "negative" because it causes you to correct—back to your idea of how things are supposed to be.

This negative tension comes whenever you're out of your comfort zone. You sense this anxiety whenever your environment or behavior doesn't match your internal construct of how things are supposed to be. This tension or anxiety causes a loss of memory; it shuts down your recall of knowledge, names, skills. You act as if you don't know what is happening to you. The information is inside you, but you can't retrieve it because you're off the beam.

That anxiety not only limits your recall, it also blocks input. Somebody could be telling you how to get somewhere, but if you think that you're out of your comfort zone, you block the input of information. Sadly, you mistake that inability to receive and recall information as a lack of potential or ability. You say, "Oh, I must be dumb at this." You say, "Oh, I don't have the aptitude for this." But you're probably just out of place for you, out of your comfort zone, and so you make the wrong conclusion about the use and the development of the potential you have inside yourself.

One way to release your wonderful potential is to learn how to control anxiety arousal to handle the pressure of being outside your comfort zone. Another way is to increase your efficacy. We need an army of efficacious people with heart. Efficacy just means to cause and make happen—the power to cause and make happen what you want to make happen. You'll want to, too, when you find out why. You'll want to because it will give you more power, more depth, more satisfaction. It doesn't do you any good to gain money or to accumulate power if inside you're not proud of yourself.

As you increase your efficacy, you will see bigger and better ideals, and more options and possibilities, where presently you can't see them. That's because you know "the truth" of your situation. But I can see it in my mind. It's a vision. It's an idea and an ideal.

As you expand your comfort zone, the spiral will get bigger. You'll turn and face bigger problems. It's a constant process of growing inside, of having a bigger "there." The there that you think of today will be small compared to the there that you'll think of ten years from now, if you apply what you learn daily to develop yourself.

You can't imagine yourself doing some things you see others doing; but don't let that stop you from doing what is possible for you to do at the level you're at. You can learn how to use your imagination not only to change the goal, but to stretch your comfort zone. That's part of the goal-setting process, internally changing or stretching your idea of where you belong by using your forethought and your imagination constructively. As you internally expand where you belong, you allow yourself to move in that direction without that negative feedback causing you to go back to "being yourself."

5. Create a team of people around you. These are people who, in their own way, can do whatever they need to do to build that community or that environment toward that ideal. You recognize that one person can't do it alone. And so you seek the company of soulmates who have similar ideals. As you create a team of such people around you, including your immediate family, you then experience the power of synergy. Your work will begin to have greater significance and influence.

Pass the baton on to others. Learn how to pass the baton to others—to your family, to your children, to the people around you. Learn how to be a mentor, a coach, a teacher, a leader. And allow yourself to be admired by people around you who may say, "How can I be like you?" You'll tell them, "This is how." Because you want them to experience the same joy. Remember, however, that you are not the model—only one good model. Allow people to run the race their way, their style, their methods, their ideals.

Lou Tice is chairman of The Pacific Institute. He is the author of *Smart Talk for Achieving Your Potential,* from which this article was adapted with permission.

5

Why Be and Do Good?

by Harold Kushner

We *have become* so sophisticated, so enmeshed in the trappings of the modern world, that we have been enriched in a lot of ways and impoverished in more important ways. We are so good at minimizing the domain of the gods, intruding on holy space, claiming it as our own, that we're ending up with a lot to feel proud about but nothing to inspire us. Idol worship is treating humans as if they were the ultimate.

Technology is the enemy of reverence because technology is the worship of the man-made. Ultimately, the worship of the man-made limits our ability to worship the divine. God has built standards into the world of right and wrong, of moral good and evil, that are as fixed as the laws of gravity. These things are not subject to majority vote. There are some things you simply cannot do. God has forbidden them. I am not diminished by being told there are certain things I may not do because they are wrong. Rather, following standards enhances me. It tuns me into a real human being, somebody whose deeds, whose decisions, whose choices matter at the highest level.

God cares about what you do. You cannot claim it is all right to betray your marriage and commit adultery, even if a majority of the people want it that way, anymore than you can claim winter should be mild and ice cream should be more nourishing than vegetables. There are some things that simply are there. There is something inside of me, and I suspect there is something inside every one of us, that has an instinctive response to injustice. This part of us says, "That's wrong. Don't let them get away with it." There is something in us that recognizes right and wrong. There are right ways and wrong ways to live, and they are all taken very seriously by Him. This endows every waking hour of our lives with meaning. If you know that certain things are wrong and you do them anyway, you need radical forgiveness, a sense of cleansing from the sense of inadequacy, from the knowledge you have not been the kind of person you should be.

I have learned that whatever I think of myself, God thinks better of me. No matter how much you've messed up your life, God still cares about you. God loves us despite all our failings. We have to go out and love ourselves and love our families despite their failings the way God loves us.

I know there is part of me that is not physical, a part that I call my soul, or spirit. It is everything about me that is non-physical; my identity, my values, my memories, my sense of humor. Now, because it is not physical, it is not subject to death. My soul cannot die. That is not a religious dogma, that is a sci-entific fact. It can't be argued with. A soul is immortal because a soul is nonphysical and not subject to death.

Hell is the understanding that if I am sarcastic to my daugh-ter, she will be sarcastic to my grandchildren, and it will be my fault. Hell is realizing that every time I tell a lie because the truth is embarrassing, I am voting to make this a more deceitful world for my family to live in.

Heaven is the awareness that every time I do something good, even if nobody thanks me for it, and every time I resist temptation, the world is permanently better for the good that I do.

If there is not God, who is there to inspire us? Who is there to guide us? Who is there to pick us up and wipe us off when we've fallen and dirtied ourselves? And who is there to replenish our love and our hope and our strength when we've used it up? And who is there to promise that what we have not finished in our life-time will be finished in a later lifetime because He will link one life to another? If there is no God, we are all by ourselves in this uni-verse and it is too big and too vast and too cold for us to run.

So, who needs God? I know I do. And I know we do.

Rabbi Harold S. Kushner is Rabbi Laureate of Temple Israel in Natick, Massachusetts and author of *When Bad Things Happen to Good People.*

6

Winner's Edge

by Denis Waitley

If you can't see yourself doing something or achieving something, you literally cannot do it! It's not what you are that holds you back, it's what you think you're not.

Six self-directed keys will give you an edge in winning against the toughest of all competition—a negative self-image.

1. Living without limitations (positive self-awareness). You can learn to live without limitations. Limits are physical boundaries, but imitations are psychological barriers, such as feeling unworthy of material success or happiness. So, avoid judging yourself against the fantasies presented by television commercials and motion pictures. Reality says you have the potential to become infinitely more than you are now. You can develop abilities through observation, imitation and reasoning. The greatest limitations you will ever face will be those you place on yourself. Others may rain on your parade, but you don't have to take on the role of victim. You can rewrite your scenario and become a victor in life. You are your own scriptwriter, and the play is never finished, no matter what your age, position, or station in life.

2. Deserving to win (positive self-esteem). You want to say, "I like myself. I'd rather be me than anyone else in the world." With positive self-talk, you can have a strong sense of self-worth, regardless of your status. Learned to like yourself. Instead of comparing yourself to others, view yourself in terms of your own abilities, interests, and goals. You always project on the outside how you feel on the inside. Self-acceptance is the key to healthy self-esteem—seeing yourself as an imperfect but worthwhile, changing, and growing individual. Although we aren't born with equal talent, we are born with the equal right to feel deserving of excellence according to our own internal standards.

3. The proactive person (positive self-determination). Losers let it happen. Winners make it happen. Life is a do-it-yourself project. Whatever you give credence to in your thinking will likely come to pass. Learn to develop two critical capabilities: the ability to live with uncertainty, and the ability to delay immediate gratification in favor of long-range goals. Losers try to escape from their fears with activities that are tension-relieving. Winners are motivated by their desires toward activities that are goal-achieving.

Choose your responses to what occurs. Learn from your mistakes, rather than repeat them. Spend time taking action in the present, rather than fearing what may happen in the future.

Be different, if it means higher personal and professional standards. Be different, if it means being cleaner, neater, and better groomed. Be different, if it means putting more time and effort into all you do. And be different, if it means taking the calculated risk. The greatest risk in life is to wait for and depend upon others for your own security. The greatest security is to plan and act, and take the risk that will ultimately make you independent.

4. The gold mine (positive self-direction). You have a gold mine in your goal mind. Goals are like gold. Thoughts and dreams are like ore. Until the ore is extracted, shaped and given form, it has little value. Most people never reach their goals because they never set them in the first place. They spend more time planning a vacation than they do planning their own lives. The mind is like a guidance system. Once a goal is set, the mind constantly monitors self-talk and feedback, making adjustments along the way to reach its target. Purpose is the engine that powers our lives. If we keep focused on our purpose and the desired result, we can move through routines, details, delays, and around or over any obstacles in our path. Specific written goals, both for our professional and personal lives, are the tools that make purpose achievable. Most of us are good at setting professional goals, but often we leave our personal lives to the luck of the draw. Since the mind is a marvelous biocomputer, it needs specific instructions. Winners know where they are going, and they get there.

5. The victor's circle (positive self-talk). The "vicious circle" is where one problem gives rise to another, leading back to the first problem and magnifying it. The "victor's circle" is where one success gives rise to another success, which is parlayed into an even greater success. Positive self-talk, before and after performance, is an important key to the permanent enhancement of self-esteem and goal achievement.

Our self-image has been built by our own beliefs and thoughts about ourselves. It records our self-talk minute to minute. This running commentary has a powerful effect on your performance. We all talk to ourselves in words, pictures, and emotions at 300 to 400 words a minute. Every waking moment we mold our self-image with thoughts about ourselves and our performance. Become aware of your silent conversations. You are constantly judging and prejudging every action. Your self-talk is creating your self-image and your goals. The most important briefings, meetings, and conversations you'll ever have are the ones you'll have with yourself. It isn't enough to want success. It's not enough to plan it. It's not enough to act on it. You must think it, see it, and say it—every minute of your life.

6. The eagle's vision (positive self-dimension). As we enter the 21st century, innovators and visionaries will replace the predators and intimidators. Independence will be replaced by interdependence. The winners will be champions of cooperation rather than tooth-and-claw competition. The most competitive force is to always give more in the service you render than you expect to receive. Rising expectations of developing nations and consumers make it mandatory that we never rest on our past laurels or take success for granted.

The eagle is the symbol for quiet power and scope. We must open our lenses, like the eagle, to see the forest and the trees, and to spot opportunities to create synergy by joining individual parts of our lives to make a greater, more dynamic whole person—a person who understands the meaning of team and time.

Winners live by the win-win ethic because their security is not based on externals. If your self-esteem is based on externals, your work or your wealth is your worth; a setback becomes a failure; someone else's win means your loss; and if you aren't number one, then you're no good. But for true champions, a loss is a learning experience; and failure, like fertilizer, makes things grow faster in the future. Over time, good seeds, planted in good soil, yield fruit.

If you have internal strength, external setbacks won't keep you down very long.

Denis Waitley, author of *The Psychology of Winning, Seeds of Greatness, The Winner's Edge, The Double Win, Being the Best,* and *Empires of the Mind,* is chairman of Denis Waitley, Inc.

7

Get Ego Out of the Way

by Monica L. Simons

have found that one thing disrupts forward progress more than anything—the ego. My own experience of the ego is that it wants the good life. The ego does not like pain, but demands instant gratification. As Clarissa Pinkola Estes, Ph.D. explains in *Women Who Run with the Wolves,* "There are three things that differentiate living from the soul versus living from the ego only: the ability to sense and learn new ways, the tenacity to ride a rough road, and the patience to learn deep love over time."

When I want a quick fix, I am operating out of my ego. When I cannot walk the talk, but can dictate it to others, I am being ego-centered. And when I want a lasting solution, I am not going to find one, as long as I am stuck in my ego.

The greatest thing a person can do is to continually assess his or her own performance and make continual improvements. In other words, walk the talk. Don't ask that of me that you are unwilling to do yourself. If you are a pot, don't call the kettle black. Show me how to grow through your own growth. Guide me through the maze, but don't try to change me. Because, anytime we try to control another human being, we will always find ourselves dealing with rebellion.

Hold a mirror up to yourself every day and say, "What do I need to look at today? Am I doing the things that I have committed to doing? And if not, why not? What is blocking me? Is it some sort of obstacle, is it another person, is it my own fear?" This is the process that propels real growth and transformation.

However, this is the process that the ego hates most because the ego wants to stay safe and comfortable. "Let's focus on someone else today," says the ego, "so that my cozy little world can remain intact."

Consider a caterpillar that goes into a cocoon. If it stayed there forever, we would never see that beautiful butterfly emerge. And the same holds true with soul. As long as the ego runs that show, we never get to see the real person emerge, including all the wonderful gifts that each and every one of us possesses. Instead, they get covered up by shame, fear, and ego.

We need to get our egos out of the way so our real selves can emerge. But for that to happen, it takes hard work. I like to think of it as "psychic" housekeeping. We have many rooms inside our psyche that are chambers for all of our truths and life experiences. These events have become part of our subconscious and tend to motivate our response to life.

Past trauma can program our responses to life. If these events were dysfunctional in any shape or form, it is possible that we may need to reevaluate some of our belief systems and see if they are valid or if they are based on the messages that resulted from our trauma.

The only way to change these behaviors and our reactions is to do our own "psychic" housekeeping, which can be quite painful and not at all appealing to the ego. However, it is the only way to let the soul emerge in situations where the ego is predominant. And whether we actively choose to work through an issue or fate deals us an opportunity to face it head on, we will always be better off for having done so. Your ego may not think so, but your soul will.

Soul Characteristics

The following list describes what I believe are true characteristics of the soul:

1. Patience to let things unfold. In other words, let things follow a process versus trying to control outcomes. This is where most of our growth and learning comes from—the process undertaken, not the end result. In fact, outcomes sometimes do not occur until we have mastered the lessons of the process. And if you are not feeling clear on a situation, let go of outcomes and trust that the process will eventually lead you to clarity.

2. *Acceptance of situations.* We need not stay "hooked" into a situation. We may decide that the only way we can accept a situation is to exit—that it is time for us to move on. In doing so, we are able to realize and honor that we may have different beliefs than those involved in the situation. This doesn't mean that we are right and they are wrong or vice versa. It simply means that today, at this point in time, we are willing to accept that we disagree. And perhaps down the road, we may see things differently, but right now we are staying true to our own needs.

3. *Willingness to look closely at self and be committed to changing "ego-based" behaviors.* This is the psychic housekeeping that I referred to earlier. And there is not one "right" way to do this. I have seen many people arrive at the same conclusion yet take many different paths to get there. It is important to honor your own process of learning. The key thing of importance is to be able to identify those areas that need evaluation. John Gray, Ph.D., has a saying "what you name, you can change," as well as a book entitled *What You Feel, You Can Heal*. Enough said.

4. *Belief in a Higher Power, the self and others.* To heal our egos, we need to believe in something much greater than ourselves. Then, we need to believe that we are a part of the greatness and recognize that we all come from the same place; that we all have unlimited potential to excel, to succeed, to self-actualize. Without this belief, we limit our own growth potential. We will get so far and then hit a wall.

At this point in time, we possess all that we will ever need; however, it often takes a lifetime to figure that out and to realize our own self-worth. We realize that the Divine Mystery is willing to offer us great abundance, yet we often cut off the very source that can supply us with the things that we so desperately want in our lives. Many of us are not afraid of our own shadow, but rather our own light. Because, somewhere deep inside of every one of us, that light burns brighter than anything we could ever imagine—and in doing so, it can scare the life out of us so we stay stuck hidden in our shadow.

5. *Simplicity.* We need the ability to keep things short, sweet and simple, to allow ourselves to be clear and concise. When we find that we need to explain something in many different ways, it may be an indicator that something remains unresolved within us.

When we find it difficult to operate out of the soul, it is usually an indication that our ego and defense mechanisms are running the show. When this occurs, it is important to be gentle in this acknowledgement. We need to learn to love and embrace our shadow, especially since there is usually a reason why our ego has taken over in the first place. This reason may not be apparent at first, but after some emotional exploration, it usually becomes much clearer. And without love and compassion, we make the healing process much more difficult.

6. *Transformation.* Transforming the ego takes time. It may not always feel like we are growing. But if we were to make a list of all that we would like to change and review that list in six months, we would most likely notice our growth. However, if we listen to the ego, the ego is already focused on what else is wrong and is looking for an immediate solution.

When we dwell on our problems, we can't acknowledge the solutions and growth that have taken place. It is important to celebrate our growth. This doesn't mean we abandon any future growth, but it means taking time to see the whole spectrum of colors that appear with our transformation.

According to mandala expert Lori Jo Scheel, "When white light passes through a prism, there is more than just white light. There is an entire rainbow of colors, just waiting to be noticed," which is much more interesting than the pot, the kettle, and the color black.

Monica L. Simons is an independent business consultant.

8

The Puzzle of Personal Excellence

Dianna Booher

I've been trying to put together the puzzle of personal excellence, and I want to share what I've learned so far—sometimes through painful experience. My goal is to help you create your own *Plan for Personal Excellence*—a 14-point plan that may mark a turning point in your life and career.

1. Define success in your own terms. Picture yourself sitting at your dining room table about to put together a jigsaw puzzle. What do you do first? You look at the picture on the box. And in creating your own *Personal Excellence Plan*, you do the same thing: You picture in your mind what success looks like for you.

Too many of us measure our success by what others have or haven't done. Too many of us have only a vague idea of what we ultimately want in life. And even if we can state it, we don't translate that belief to our daily work and decisions.

Decide how you'll measure your own success. Write an axiom you want to live by. Repeat it to yourself often. That will help you translate success into everyday decisions. To me, quality of life means control of your life. Your definition of success will help you control your life by controlling how you make decisions.

2. Assess your strengths. Why do we find it hard to tell others of our strengths? Well, our mothers taught us not to brag, to be modest, and to let others point out our virtues. When my children were growing up, psychologists were emphasizing the importance of building a child's self-esteem. One day my kindergartner climbed into the car and, very bubbly, began to show me her artwork for the day. Then she added proudly, "My teacher said it was the best one in the class. I'm good at staying in the lines when I color. In fact, I can't think of anything I'm not good at." She looked at me smugly. I didn't want to burst her bubble. She'd become aware of the failures soon enough.

That admonition not to brag can overshadow our need to get focused on what we do best. Whatever your talents and strengths, take an honest assessment. See what you have to work with, and look for opportunities to build on those strengths.

3. Set goals with deadlines. If you're sailing and you don't have any plans to go anyplace special, then any wind is the right wind. But if you have a certain port you want to make by noon, then you need to pick a specific direction and find the right wind.

The biggest goal I ever set for myself was to become a full-time writer. I soon learned that talk is cheap. Goals are just "pie in the sky" dreams until they have deadlines. In addition to goals and deadlines, you need a plan of action. If you plan to switch careers, what new training will you need? Where can you get it? What financing do you need? Who should you know?

Successful individuals have specific goals, deadlines, and action plans. A good test of your goals is to ask yourself: "How much excitement do my goals generate?" Don't be afraid to show your commitment about reaching a goal.

After you reach one goal, raise the bar and "start over" in pursuit of your new goal. Winners expect to win in advance. Life, for them, becomes a self-fulfilling prophecy. Choice, not chance, determines destiny. Make some choices. Set some goals. Add deadlines. Make plans and take action.

4. Develop discipline and be willing to pay the price. Today's preparation determines tomorrow's achievement. No one has cornered the market on family and career success. Anybody who pays the price can walk out with it.

To excel in your chosen field, find out what it takes to be the best—time, practice, commitment, sacrifice. There is a price. Success is never on sale; it's just a matter of deciding how much you want to pay. After deciding, it's a matter of doing.

Emerson said that our primary need in life is somebody who will make us do what we can. At some time, we've all had that somebody—a parent, friend, teacher. But as adults, we have to be that somebody ourselves.

We need the discipline to realize our potential, to keep up in our field, to use our time well, to eat right and stay healthy, and to stay with a task to completion. Follow-through marks success. Self-discipline is simply control. If you don't control yourself, someone else will—or no one else will. Either case will be less desirable than self-control. You can't always control the circumstances, but you can control your reaction or response.

5. Use time wisely. My time management philosophy is this: "Life's short; do what counts first." I picked up the idea from the story about steel magnate Charles Schwabb. Each day he made a list of things that needed to be done. Then he added a priority number on those items. Every day he started with item number one and worked on that until he finished it. Then he went to item two, and so forth.

Thomas Edison made the most of his time by taking short naps to rejuvenate himself when working almost around the clock. Do you spend your minutes as wisely as your money? How you decide to spend your time means the difference between success and failure.

6. Ask for advice. There's a lot of wisdom and expertise out there for free if you're willing to ask. People love to do you favors—even your enemies. I learned that bit of wisdom from Benjamin Franklin. In the senate, he frequently found himself up against an archrival who owned a printing business that competed with his. Constantly, the competitor harangued him until Ben Franklin determined to make the man a friend. His plan? He learned the man had a rare book collection, so he went to his home and asked to borrow a certain book from his collection. Franklin took the book home and kept it for one week, and then returned it to the owner. Forever after, the man became his friend. Why? People love to do favors for people. When you humble yourself to ask their advice, you compliment them for their expertise. And you yourself, of course, grow from their wisdom and knowledge. Asking people for advice, for opinions, for their expertise, helps you and compliments them.

7. Be receptive to feedback. Some "advice" you don't ask for. That's what I call feedback—unsolicited opinions about you or your work. Those comments are sometimes more valuable than what you do ask for. We tend to ask for guidance—and we want it to be positive. Feedback is usually unsolicited and often unfavorable. But it can be most valuable, even if embarrassing.

Granted, you can get too much negative or contradictory feedback and become discouraged. But feedback, properly evaluated, from a caring contributor can be invaluable in gaining perspective on where you're going.

We need to measure ourselves with someone else's yardstick occasionally. If you're getting the same feedback from several sources—either positive or negative—pay attention.

8. Stay informed. Chief Justice Oliver Wendell Holmes said, "Man's mind, once stretched by a new idea, never regains its original dimensions." When I started my consulting and training business, I read everything I could find on the subject. Only high school seniors know it all. The rest of us have to read and learn.

When a U.S. team traveled to Japan in the 1980s to study the Toyota production system and the innovative Japanese just-in-time concept, they met with the system's creator, Taiichi Ohno. When the Americans questioned him about what inspired his thinking, he laughed, "I learned it all from Henry Ford's book." The book he referred to was *Today and Tomorrow*, written by Ford and published by Doubleday in 1926. Leaders are readers.

Someone has said of us knowledge-workers, "Wealth was once measured in gold. Now it's measured in what we know." Stay alert and informed. Read voraciously.

9. Learn to communicate well. Management guru Peter Drucker says your career success and salary over a lifetime will be more directly related to your writing and speaking skills than to any technical expertise you have. The whole world is in a mess because we don't communicate well. Students don't listen to teachers. Politicians don't listen to taxpayers. Suppliers don't listen to customers. The result is miscommunication—between management and employees, between marketing and accounting, between service and sales.

Communication skills—both talking and writing—create an impression and either clarify or confuse. I once received a letter from a stockbroker, wanting me to switch my IRA funds to his company. He had four misspelled words and a sentence fragment in his letter. Do you think I'd trust him with my money? How do I know he'd get it in the right account? In whatever field or relationship, your communication skills make an impression. And they either cost money or make money. Either you get the job done or you don't. You get what you want, or you don't.

10. *Do quality work.* Sometimes the only difference between failure and success is doing something almost right and doing it exactly right. At best, shoddy work—inattention to detail and mistakes—irritates people; at worst, it destroys personal credibility and endangers lives. Real quality in a product or service boils down to individual work. It's always personal.

In this age of "Preferred Vendor" lists, organizations rate how well their vendors perform on each sale. Are they responsive when you phone? Do their invoices have errors? Are their deliveries on time? If organizations are keeping their eyes on their vendors in such a manner, they're certainly aware of the quality of work being done by their own employees.

Quality is worth the effort. Mistakes and inattention to detail can cause serious harm. So, care enough to do quality work. Pay attention to the detail. Do things right the first time. After every project, ask yourself, "Would I stake my personal reputation on this work? Would I bet someone's life on it?" Customers, employers, family, and friends deserve your best.

11. *Take risks.* Nothing gets the adrenaline pumping like risk-taking. When I quit my teaching job to start my consulting business, I wasn't taking a big risk because I knew I could always find another teaching job. The big risk for me was buying a wardrobe. That meant taking money out of the bank. We each have our own way of evaluating risk. I took risks inch-by-inch.

Now my risks with a larger company and employees dependent on me are a little larger. Nevertheless, they're necessary. Whatever worthwhile goal you plan to achieve, you'll have to take risks. Whether it's risking the time to do an interview, pay tuition to a seminar, spend time researching, or move across country—risk is the bridge you'll have to cross.

12. *Be dependable.* Under what circumstances do you waffle about commitments you've made? All you have to do to be considered excellent in many circles is simply to do what you say you will. There's a bittersweet truth in that fact. Being dependable used to be a mediocre reference—something you said about people when you couldn't think of anything more praiseworthy. Now, being dependable states an outstanding accomplishment. Daniel Webster said: "The most important thought that ever entered my mind is my personal accountability to Almighty God."

13. Be ethical. We have to know when to compromise and when to stick to our convictions. What you and I once knew to be right and wrong is still right and wrong. There is such a thing as wrong. Plagiarism among politicians, preachers, or students is wrong. Lying on resumes is wrong. Copying videos, audiotapes, or disks without permission is wrong.

If you want a real picture of the state of the world, notice the reaction of those who see you act honestly and responsibly—it may amaze and shock them. When honesty shocks people, society needs a new perspective. To be perceived as excellent, be ethical.

14. Nurture relationships. You want to know how to have some fun every day of your life? Confucius said, "Choose a job you love, and you will never have to work a day in your life." For the most part, he was right. My job is mostly fun, but every job has its days of drudgery. So on those days, learn to play at something else. Have fun improving your interactions with people around you—your colleagues, your customers, your friends.

Thoreau said: "A friend is someone with whom you may think aloud." The greatest tragedy is not having more friendships. Everybody needs to laugh and love with family and friends. We all need to keep our balance and our sanity. It helps to have positive interactions, transactions, and relationships.

By putting all these pieces of the puzzle in place, you'll see the whole picture of personal excellence—and you'll make a difference in the world. Review your personal plan for excellence often. Keep it in a prominent place as a daily reminder. Personal excellence doesn't have to be a puzzle at all. To make a difference, just do it—dream, dare, and do it.

Dianna Booher is CEO of Booher Consultants, a communications training firm.

9

How to Get What You Want Out of Life

by Dr. Joyce Brothers

When *I was* in the fourth grade, I wanted only three things out of life: the best marks in my class, a blue velvet dress with a white-lace collar to wear to birthday parties, and to be the best roller skater on the block. By the time I was in high school, I wanted a lot more. My parents, both lawyers, encouraged me to aim high. At one point I announced that I had decided to be a nurse when I grew up. "A nurse!" my mother said in disbelief. "Why not be a doctor?" Why not, indeed?

And I did become a doctor—a psychologist and Doctor of Philosophy, not of medicine (I married one of those). Like most girls at that time, I wanted a happy marriage and a family more than anything else. I was fortunate enough to marry a wonderful man, a husband who is as pleased with my successes as he is with his own, even after more than a quarter of a century of marriage. Our daughter, Lisa, has grown up to be a woman I respect—and my very good friend as well. And I have a career that allows me to do what I enjoy most in the world: help people understand themselves better.

Some people tell me that I'm lucky, but I shake my head. I don't believe in luck. We make our own good fortune. It certainly was not luck that helped me win "The $64,000 Question"—something that gave a whole new direction to my life. At the time, I wanted a Cadillac more than anything else in the world. Milt and I used to sit in front of our television set every Tuesday night watching "The $64,000 Question," the most popular program of the era. "What does anyone do with $64,000?" we asked each other. What must it feel like to be rich beyond belief?

Well, I passed the goal I had originally set for myself: that Cadillac. And then one night I won. Won the Sixty-Four!

This was a watershed experience for me, the first time I had gone all out, giving up everything else in my life to get what I wanted. And it changed the whole direction of my life. I knew what it was to work and work hard, but I had never worked so intensely before, never had such total commitment. I had pushed my energies and my brain and my emotions to the limit, to the point where it hurt—and it paid off. In so many ways. I was asked to appear on radio and television shows, to lecture, to write. And I took to it the way a duck takes to water.

Six months earlier, I had thought I wanted a Cadillac more than anything else in the world. Now I knew better. I wanted the fame and fun and money of this world of mass communications. And now I understood that I could use my knowledge of psychology, of people's reactions and interactions, motivations and needs to help me get what I wanted. And I did. You can too.

I do not mean to set myself up as a textbook example of success. Like everyone else, I have experienced failure—and tried to learn from it. This experience was the chief source of my interest in how people get what they want out of life—and how they determine just what it is they want. Over the years, I have observed people who have solid, happy marriages, people who manage vast enterprises, people who perform pioneering surgery, people who have become very rich, people who are world-famous, and people who lead quiet, happy lives.

I have followed the research on motivation and manipulation, on energy levels and degrees of commitment. I have advised large corporations how to get what they want and schoolchildren on how to get what they want. And I have come to the conclusion that the person who truly knows what he or she wants out of life and who is willing to work for it will achieve that goal. The first—and most important—step is to find out what you really want. Not what you think you should or what someone else thinks you should, but what you, the inner you, really wants out of life.

Dr. Joyce Brothers is a renowned psychologist whose audience numbers in the millions. She is the author of many best-selling books.

10

The Winner's Attitude

by Vince Lombardi

Have *you ever* wondered whether winners share a common attitude, or whether winners have certain thought patterns in common? They do, and one of these thought patterns is:

The will to win, the will to achieve, goes dry and arid without constant reinforcement.

Throughout history, winners and heroes have experienced periods in their lives that could be described as their desert experiences, when they've been confused and discouraged. Why, therefore, does it come as a surprise to us when we experience similar times in our lives? Times that are dry and arid, when we feel discouraged, times of stress when events in our lives are taking place so fast that we don't know the questions, much less the answers.

Life is difficult! And what a disservice we do to our young people if we don't impart this message to them, and soon. Life is difficult, but it doesn't have to be hard. Life comes to us in a series of challenges, and the attitude with which we choose to perceive these challenges and the mind-set with which we prepare for these challenges determines whether our lives are hard or whether our lives are rewarding.

Viktor Frankl, a Jewish psychiatrist, spent World War II in a concentration camp, and in that camp he lost his wife, his child and a manuscript that was his life's work. While in the camp, Frankl became fascinated with the question of why some people in the difficult circumstances of a concentration camp quickly gave up and died and why others not only survived but some grew stronger. From his observations, Frankl concluded that it was attitude—how people chose to perceive their experience—that made the difference. Frankl continued, "Everything can be taken from a man but one thing: the last of human freedoms, the ability to choose one's attitude in any given set of circumstances, to choose one's own way."

What's the key to acquiring the kind of attitude that allows people to survive a concentration camp and allows you and I to live lives that are rewarding?

The key is constant reinforcement. A trap so many of us fall into is that when we see or hear something that affects our attitude in a positive or constructive manner, we say to ourselves, "That's it, I've got it" and we go about our business. It doesn't work that way. We aren't made that way.

The truth can be expressed in many ways. The truth that inspires and moves and encourages us wears many faces. It's been observed that outside of the Bible, Emerson and Shakespeare, very little has been written or expressed that's original. You have only to go to your favorite bookstore and check out the self-help section to understand there's more than one way to say basically the same thing. But what may click for you may leave me cold. Maybe you would rather listen to a tape, whereas I learn better reading a book. The critical point is, we need to spend time every day listening to tapes, reading books and surrounding ourselves with people we can learn from. And what we're shooting for with this constant reinforcement is that eventually we will begin to internalize the winner's attitude.

Have you ever wondered why successful coaches put so much emphasis on practice? They run the same plays over and over and over until the players can execute those plays in their sleep, and that's exactly what the coaches want! At the crucial moment in big games, coaches can't have players thinking about their next move. If players have to think, it's probably too late. They've got to act and react appropriately, without thinking, so moves must be second nature to them. The next move must be so internalized that it's instinctive and habitual.

It's the same for you and me. Things are happening so fast today that we don't have time to stop and do an attitude check every time we're faced with a problem. If we have to think, we miss an opportunity. The winner's mind-set must be internalized through the constant reinforcement of reading books, listening to tapes and associating with people we can grow with, so that we will respond to our next challenge, instinctively and habitually.

One important aspect of this constant reinforcement is the questions we ask ourselves: "Am I going to allow my life to be governed by daily activities, or do I choose to live my life in accordance with noble principles?" It's been said that questions are the source of all knowledge.

In other words, am I just reacting to life, or am I living my life in a proactive manner? Am I so busy putting out fires that I don't have time to start any? Am I allowing my life to be governed by outside forces, or am I choosing to live my life in accordance with decisions I'm making? Do I have important goals and dreams that I am committed to, or am I creatively avoiding commitments by filling my life with daily activities?

Only you can choose the attitude you want to internalize and the principles you want to live by, but here's something to think about: Do you remember the PBS program "The Power of Myth," that consisted of a conversation between Bill Moyers and Joseph Campbell? Joseph Campbell was a scholar whose field of expertise was mythology. Part of their conversation touched on the "hero's journey," a common theme in mythology. Campbell contrasted the celebrity with the hero. The celebrity is ego driven; the hero is motivated to serve others. The celebrity lives for self, the hero gives of self. We have lots of celebrities in Hollywood, Washington, D.C., on Wall Street, Madison Avenue and in professional sports, don't we? Too many of us look to celebrities to see how we should act and what principles and values we should live by.

We need heroes today, heroes to pull us together into some kind of common intention, some kind of common purpose. We need heroes to suggest new possibilities to us or reintroduce us to some old ones. While life can be rewarding, it can also be difficult. Yet the hero courageously pursues the journey, acting in the service of others.

Campbell urged everyone to find their bliss and follow it. And in doing so, by just being fully alive and aware, like the athlete who for that brief moment finds his or her center or zone where everything goes right, heroes do their part to redeem the world. "The influence of a vital person, vitalizes," said Campbell.

The "hero's journey" doesn't necessarily involve moving mountains. We can be heroes at home, at work or in our communities. And it is through the constant reinforcement of the winner's attitude that we can all become heroes.

Vince Lombardi is a popular speaker and seminar leader.

SECTION 2

Performance

11

Four Principles

by Steve Young

A *"principle" is a* basic truth, law, or moral standard. Principles then, should be timeless. We should feel confident in the fact that while circumstances may change, new challenges may arise, and the very world may change, true principles will stand. So, what could be more valuable than discovering, understanding, and living true principles?

I'd like to share what I accept as four principles of truth:

1. A strong work ethic, over time, will lead to success. I can see in myself a work ethic which I believe has come through past generations, and has been nurtured by my immediate family and by my football family. I grew up in a home where a pioneer work ethic, along with other principles and values, was taught to me and modeled for me by my parents. I now see a direct correlation between that personal work ethic and my success today as a professional athlete. My father was a strict disciplinarian, and his creed was "If you're not working, how are you having any fun?" He taught us that creed by example.

I've grown up with the belief that you can be and do whatever you can imagine for yourself if you are willing to pay the price.

As the oldest child in my family and as the quarterback on football teams, I've learned to love discipline, tough situations, and hard work. You get used to it. If you drive a car 75 miles per hour long enough, when you go 55, it seems like you're crawling. You get used to the criticism and the scrutiny. You almost become comfortable with it.

2. You improve faster if you compete only with yourself, and compare your current effort only with your past performance. Today's hunger for competition leads to a belief that in every aspect of life, there is a champion and there are losers. This is a dangerous way to think. Everyone should be competing against himself or herself, and no one else. In football, I've learned from people like Jerry Rice to compete primarily against myself—to work at being the best quarterback I can be, and to not only play to my strengths but also to work on my weaknesses.

3. Center your life on God. I've been able to put everything in perspective the last couple of years. Now when something comes in and hits me, it doesn't go all the way to the center. I think that's because my life is not centered on what others think of me. I have something else at the center of my life. Don't waste your time worshipping sports heroes, rock stars, movie idols, or CEOs. Please, just worship God, your Heavenly Father.

Turn to Him in faith; let Him take you by the hand and lead you through this life. He will not let you down. I have come to understand that life's whole process is a walk in faith. It is faith that prepares you for that next experience. It is faith that makes you understand clearly that there is something to learn from every experience. And faith reassures you that there is life beyond your current activity.

4. Be united, having a sense of family. If we are to build a successful team, family, or community we have to do it on the principle of oneness. If we work for the good of all, we will achieve beyond our dreams. The principle of unity rings true because it is based on timeless principles of personal responsibility, leadership, and loyalty to "family" members.

Working with my father, I noticed he showed the same respect to everyone. Through his example I observed that this feeling of "family" can and should extend throughout the entire community.

In addition to my family, I have in a very real sense, a football family. On our team, we apply the principles of family: leadership, personal responsibility, and commitment to each other.

In 1987 I joined the San Francisco 49ers; upon my arrival in the city, I was invited to meet with the 49er owner Edward DeBartolo. When I entered his office and shook his hand, he said, "Welcome to the family." He ran his organization with a "sense of family." He demanded premium effort, respect for your teammates through finding common ground and understanding, and sacrifice for the common good of the team.

Selflessness is the key to the success of any team because by working together we can symbiotically and synergistically create more than just the sum of our parts.

I was involved in a championship effort which resulted in a Super Bowl title. The feeling in the locker room was a feeling of total joy—a depth of joy that could only be experienced by those who had struggled and even failed along the way. The experience was all the more rewarding because it was shared with a team that achieved success together.

I believe that we, the generation of the information boom, must create a worldwide sense of family based on the same principles: mutual respect, selflessness, and love.

I believe that God is giving us the assignment to create this sense of family beyond the borders of our homes, cities, states, and nations—to include all people of the world, with no thought of prejudice with respect to race, religion, or government.

That melting pot effect of the supersonic age is evident in the 49ers. We are from every corner of the United States, rich and poor, and we must come together or fall. We must constantly be searching for common ground. We have to learn tolerance for our individual differences, because if we fail to bring a "sense of family" to our team it shows in front of millions of people.

That is why I support the Olympic ideals: *Citius, Altius, Fortius*—the concepts of fair play, respect for self and for others, and perhaps the greatest of all, that through sport, even warring nations might lay down their arms and come together, if only for a time, and see each other in a new way.

Wouldn't it be wonderful if that ideal could permeate our hearts and souls in a more lasting way? Perhaps one day we will realize that those moments of learning or friendly competition or international friendship are available to us every day.

Steve Young is quarterback of the San Francisco 49ers. This article was adapted from his speech to the U.N. International Year of the Family Conference.

12

Olympic Dreams

by Les Brown

Hundreds of Olympic athletes have not only lived their dreams, they have spiked our dreams too with their courage and accomplishments. The Olympic Games are perhaps the world's greatest and most dramatic stage for those in pursuit of lifelong goals and dreams. The Olympics are as much an artistic as an athletic event, for the pursuit of dreams is the art of living life as it should be lived—fully, enthusiastically, with every breath you take.

We take great inspiration from our Olympians, not just from the strength of their bodies, but from the strength of their characters. The strength of character that enabled, for example, Jesse Owens, Jackie Joyner-Kersee and Dan Jansen to endure incredible sacrifices, pain, and labor before and during their actual Olympic events is even more awesome than their incredibly tuned athletic skills and powerful physiques. We often fail to consider how many defeats these athletes had to endure before the victories began to come. How much pain preceded victory? How much sacrifice paved the way for success? It is not the Olympics that makes these individuals champions. It is the determination that brought them here that sets them apart.

Work Toward Your Dream

Everybody should have a dream, said Jesse Owens, the grandson of a slave and son of an Arkansas sharecropper. Everybody should work toward that dream. And if we believe hard enough, whether it be in the Olympic Games, the business world, the music world, or the educational world, it all comes down to one thing. One day we can all stand atop the victory stand, watching our flag rise above all others to the crescendo of our national anthem. And one day, we can say, "On this day, I am a champion."

I, too, come from very humble origins and grew up determined to rise above the circumstances of my birth. My twin brother, Wesley, and I were abandoned as infants in a vacant building in an impoverished neighborhood in Miami. We were found and adopted by Mamie Brown, a devoted and loving woman who worked as a maid, field hand and cook to raise us on her own.

Mamie, who died recently, had always wanted someone in this world to love and, believe me, she worked hard to realize her dream of having a family. She taught my brother and me a great deal about working for a dream. Many times in my life I called upon the lessons she passed on through her perseverance and hard work. I needed to.

As a boy, I was placed in classes for the mentally handicapped. Perhaps more than a learning disability, my problem was simply hyperactivity, but it took me years to overcome the stigma and low self-image of being called a special ed student.

I relate my personal background not because I compare myself to an Olympian, not even on my best day. I simply want to demonstrate that regular people like you and me experience aspects of the Olympic challenge in our own lives. I want to encourage you to take a different view of these great athletes as they compete on this grand, global stage. I want you to think of the many smaller, unheralded, and quiet victories that brought them to this point and consider that, while all of us may not compete on such a grand scale, we all pursue dreams. All of us have to overcome challenges along the way to becoming champions in our own right.

Les Brown is a full-time public speaker and author of *Live Your Dreams*. He is one of 20 contributors to the book *The Winning Spirit*, from which this article was adapted.

13

Creating Affluence

by Deepak Chopra

Affluence **is feeling** joy, health, happiness, and vitality in every moment of our existence. All material creation has the same origin. Nature goes to the same place to create a cluster of nebulas, a galaxy of stars, a rain forest, or a human body as it goes to create a thought.

Everything that we can see, touch, hear, taste, or smell is made from the same stuff and comes from the same source. Knowing this gives us the ability to fulfill any desire we have, acquire any material object we want, and experience fulfillment and happiness to any extent we aspire.

These principles not only relate to the creation of unlimited material wealth, but they can also be applied to fulfill any desire. They are the same principles that nature uses to create material reality out of a nonmaterial essence.

All material creation is structured out of information and energy. The impulses of energy and information that create our life experiences are reflected in our attitudes toward life.

Affluence or wealth means that one is easily able to fulfill one's desires, whatever they may be, whether they apply to the material realm or to our emotional, psychological or spiritual needs, or to the realm of relationship.

A truly wealthy person's attention is never focused on money alone. Moreover, a wealthy person never has money concerns. You may have millions of dollars in the bank, but if you think all the time about money, if you have concern about it, if you worry about getting more, about not having enough, or about losing it, then irrespective of the money you possess, you are poor.

As Oscar Wilde once said, "There is only one class of people that thinks more about money than the rich, and that is the poor. In fact, the poor can think of nothing else."

To have true wealth or affluence is to be totally carefree about everything in life, including money. True wealth consciousness is, therefore, consciousness. It is pure awareness. It is the unified field. It is the field of all possibilities.

We cannot know this field just by thinking about it because, by definition, it is transcendental to thought. We can, however, have experiential knowledge of this field by transcending to it and knowing it intimately as our own nature.

When we transcend, we know nonverbally without the use of words. We obtain knowledge directly, without the distracting intervention of spoken language. This is the value of meditation, which gives us the experience of pure Being, although the experience of pure Being is in itself an expression of pure bliss and pure joy.

The main advantage of alternating the experience of meditation with activity is that the more we dive into the field of pure Being, pure awareness, pure consciousness, the more our activity becomes infused with it. And then our activity acquires the qualities inherent in pure Being, in pure consciousness: infinite, unbounded, abundant, affluent, and immortal.

The best way to acquire knowledge of this field of pure Being is through meditation. Knowing about the qualities intellectually and putting attention on the qualities also helps, because, ultimately, whatever we experience is a result of the quality of our attention.

The universe is a big dream machine, churning out dreams and transforming them into reality, and our own dreams are inextricably woven into the overall scheme of things.

Know that deep inside you, in the innermost recesses of your heart, are the Goddesses of Knowledge and Wealth. Love them and nurture them, and every desire that you have will spontaneously blossom into form. For these Goddesses have only one desire: And that is to be born.

Deepak Chopra is the author of Creating Affluence: Wealth Consciousness in the Field of All Possibilities.

14

Quest for Freedom

by Pope John Paul II

The *quest for* freedom cannot be suppressed. It arises from a recognition of the inestimable dignity and value of a person, and it cannot fail to be accompanied by personal commitment.

Revolutions are made possible by the commitment of brave men and women inspired by a different, and ultimately more profound and powerful, vision: the vision of man as a creature of intelligence and free will, immersed in a mystery which transcends his own being and endows him with the ability to reflect, choose, and gain wisdom and virtue.

Freedom is the measure of man's dignity and greatness. Living the freedom sought by individuals is a great challenge to man's spiritual growth and to the moral vitality of nations. The basic question we must all face today is the responsible use of freedom.

Responsible Use of Freedom

Freedom is not simply the absence of tyranny or oppression. Nor is freedom a license to do whatever we like. Freedom has an inner logic which distinguishes it and ennobles it: freedom is ordered to the truth, and is fulfilled in man's quest for truth and in man's living the truth. Detached from the truth about the human person, freedom deteriorates into license in the lives of individuals, and, in political life, it becomes the caprice of the most powerful and the arrogance of power.

Far from being a limitation upon freedom or a threat to it, reference to the truth about the human persona, truth universally knowable through the moral law written on the hearts of all is, in fact, the guarantor of freedom's future.

Now is the time for new hope, which calls us to expel the paralyzing burden of cynicism from human life. Inspired by the example of all those who have taken the risk of freedom, can we not recommit ourselves also to taking the risk of peace?

It is one of the great paradoxes of our time that man, who began this century with a self-confident assertion of his coming of age and autonomy, approaches the end of the twentieth century fearful of himself and fearful for the future.

Learn to Conquer Fear

To ensure that the new millennium now approaching will witness a new flourishing of the human spirit, mediated through an authentic culture of freedom, men and women must learn to conquer fear. We must learn not to be afraid. We must rediscover a spirit of hope and a spirit of trust. Hope is not empty optimism springing from a naive confidence that the future will necessarily be better than the past. Hope and trust are the premises of responsible activity and are nurtured in that inner sanctuary of conscience where man is alone with God and thus perceives that he is not alone amid the enigmas of existence, for he is surrounded by the love of the Creator!

The politics of nations can never ignore the transcendent, spiritual dimension of the human experience, and could never ignore it without harming the cause of man and the cause of human freedom. Whatever diminishes man, whatever shortens the horizon of man's aspiration to goodness, harms the cause of freedom. To recover our hope and our trust at the end of this century of sorrows, we must regain sight of that transcendent horizon of possibility to which the soul of man aspires.

Because of the radiant humanity of Christ, nothing genuinely human fails to touch the hearts of Christians. Faith in Christ does not impel us to intolerance. On the contrary, it obliges us to engage others in a respectful dialogue. Love of Christ does not distract us from interest in others, but rather invites us to responsibility for them, to the exclusion of no one and indeed, if anything, with a special concern for the weakest and the suffering.

I am a witness to human dignity, a witness of hope, a witness to the conviction that the destiny of all nations lies in the hands of a merciful Providence.

Culture of Freedom

We must overcome our fear of the future, but we will not be able to overcome it completely unless we do so together. The answer to that fear is neither coercion nor repression, nor the imposition of one social model on the entire world. The answer to the fear is the common effort to build the civilization of love, founded on the universal values of peace, solidarity, justice, and liberty. And the soul of the civilization of love is the culture of freedom: the freedom of individuals and the freedom of nations, lived in self-giving, solidarity and responsibility. We must not be afraid of the future.

We must not be afraid of man. It is no accident that we are here. Each and every person has been created in the image and likeness of the One who is the origin of all that is. We have within us the capacities for wisdom and virtue. With these gifts, and with the help of God's grace, we can build in the next century and the next millennium a civilization worthy of the human person, a true culture of freedom.

Pope John Paul II is the Supreme Pontiff of the Roman Catholic Church.

15

You Can Do It!

by Mary Kay Ash

There are four kinds of people: those who make things happen; those who watch things happen; those who wonder what happened; and those who don't know that anything happened! From an early age, I wanted to be first on that list.

I have learned that people who do succeed are set apart by their personalities, objectives, and abilities. Specifically they have enthusiasm, purpose, discipline, determination, appreciation of others, and the willingness to work, serve, and learn.

I learned this lesson the hard way. When I was seven years old, my daddy came home from the sanatorium; and although three years of treatment had arrested his tuberculosis, he was not completely cured. During my childhood, he remained an invalid and in need of a great deal of tender, loving care.

I would come home from school and clean the house. Then I would do my homework. But I accepted this, and enjoyed it. Even though some of my duties were supposed to be too difficult for a child, nobody ever told me that. So, I just did them.

I'm sure my mother knew that my job sometimes seemed overwhelming. Because when she was through with her instructions she always added, "Honey, you can do it."

"You can do it!" is an everyday motto at Mary Kay Cosmetics. Often a woman will join us who is in desperate need of hearing this message. She may be a homemaker who has been out of the job market for years. Perhaps she never worked outside the home; and now, because of divorce or widowhood, she finds herself seeking a career. Maybe she worked long and hard in another field, never having heard words of encouragement. Whatever the reason, she needs to build her feelings of self-esteem and worth.

Sadly, most people live and die with their music still unplayed. They never dare to try. Why? Because they lack self-confidence. Women, especially, have so much untapped potential.

It makes sense for a woman to try to have everything going for her. An attractive appearance is something every woman can achieve, if she wants to do so. Often I refer to my list of "don'ts": don't whimper, cry, or pout to win a point; don't be late; don't be afraid to take a stand; and don't ever lose your control or your cool head.

There is no reason why a woman should not succeed in business. All she needs is: intuitiveness; foresight; product knowledge; market knowledge; guts; lipstick; clear judgment; a stubborn streak; and a computer.

Everything a woman touches should be ennobled. We have an obligation to add all those traits which have long been considered female—such things as honor, integrity, love, and honesty. You are God's masterpiece—make the most of it!

Mary Kay Ash is founder and chairman emeritus of Mary Kay.

16

Never Surrender Leadership

by Robert H. Schuller

T*ake charge.* Take control. And never surrender leadership. Leadership is the force that selects your dreams and sets your goals. It is the force that propels your endeavors to success.

1. Don't surrender leadership to outside forces. Leadership is not always found at the desk of the president or the chairman of the board. Too often people in top positions surrender their power to outside forces. Don't surrender leadership to forces such as property, buildings, and location. If you need to rebuild or relocate, take charge and take control. Never surrender leadership to such forces as poverty. Don't allow lack of money to determine your dreams or goals. There is always a way to raise the capital you need. There is a universal principle that always manifests itself: Money flows to good ideas; good ideas spawn other good ideas; dreams inspire creativity in money management.

2. Don't surrender leadership to faces. I've seen it happen. I've done it myself. You read an audience. You see an eyebrow raised or hear a throat being cleared. Through body language, someone suggests that he may not support you. You read on his face that he's going to criticize you. Before you know it, you have been intimidated by body language into silence and retreat. At that point you have surrendered leadership to a face.

3. Don't surrender leadership to farces. Farces are lies, masks. Often people of Asian, African, and Spanish minority groups have been taught that they are genetically or intellectually inferior. Now that's a farce, a mask, a lie!

4. Don't surrender leadership to fences. Fences are limiting concepts that you allow to influence your goals and dreams. Because of these concepts, we throw away ideas and dreams that we are sure we'll never be able to realize. They also cause us to lower our goals, with the result that we strive for and achieve far less than our capabilities.

5. Don't surrender leadership to frustrations. Some people reach a point where they just can't handle people anymore, government regulations anymore, or cash flow problems anymore. Anyone who has dreams and goals also has frustrations: Lack of time and money, high interest rates, disappointments when your best people let you down. Such frustrations can mount up, and if you surrender leadership to them you'll soon cash in, give up, throw in the towel, quit. Don't give in.

6. Don't surrender leadership to your fantasies. It's amazing. God gives you a brilliantly exciting idea, and you soon give in to negative fantasies: "I might try it and be rejected"; "People might laugh at me." If your dreams are bigger than most, if your ideas are more creative, there will be criticism, possibly ridicule. But don't create more condemnation than there really is. Don't allow yourself to indulge in negative fantasies that limit the size of your goals and stifle your creativity.

7. Don't surrender leadership to fears. All you have to do is cure yourself of one fear—the fear of failure. This will help: "I'd rather attempt something great and fail than attempt nothing and succeed." I admire people who make a commitment and stick their necks out. I admire people who try to reach the top and don't make it. Their egos will take a beating, but they have conquered their fear of trying. In doing so, they've won their biggest battles.

8. Don't surrender leadership to fatigue. Everybody runs tired once in a while. You need to know when you are running tired and then back off. Because if you don't, you are going to make some bad decisions. There are times when you should not see people or make decisions. When I'm tired I often do not see people. My wife knows when my energies are taxed, and blocks off time for renewal.

9. Don't surrender leadership to faults. Somebody comes along with a good idea only to have someone else find fault with the good idea and annihilate it. Never surrender leadership to the faults. Believe in the potential. There are problems with every idea. But problems call for polishing, not for demolition.

10. Don't surrender leadership to the facts. The problems you are facing today may be fact, not just theory. The unemployment statistics are factual. Facts, statistics, interest rates can definitely influence your life. But you can choose whether or not the influence will be beneficial or detrimental.

Dr. Carl Menninger, one of the great psychiatrists, once said, "Attitude is more important than facts." Your attitude needs to remain positive and in the control position.

11. Don't surrender leadership to frenzies. A lot of people maintain control and make the right decisions until they get into a frenzy, a frantic situation.

So, when something terrible happens or when something catastrophic is threatening, don't do anything. Just think.

12. Don't surrender leadership to the fates. There are all kinds of negative "fates" that social structures or the "stars" might try to impose upon you. Too many people allow their futures to be unnecessarily pre-determined by imaginary factors. Astrology is like fortune-telling and I don't like fortune tellers. They make too many negative statements. Never allow these people to move into the control position of your life.

13. Don't surrender leadership to forecasts. Some people constantly say, "Things are bad. They're only going to get worse." There will always be negative, cynical people who only believe life will go downhill as time goes on.

14. Don't surrender leadership to your foes. I had a lot of opposition when I assumed the leadership of the construction of the Crystal Cathedral. My opposition came from outside the congregation. Their criticisms were hard to take. But through the whole experience I learned this: Not a single opponent, not a single foe, not a single critic offered any better solution to my problem. I soon realized my foes weren't interested in solving my problems. They were not accountable.

15. Don't surrender leadership to your friends. Every time we have made a decision in this church, one or two of my best friends on the church board couldn't go along with it. Even in my marriage, my wife and I have not always agreed. Friends can give you advice. They can share with you their opinions. They should never have the final word. The only one who can make the decision and live with the results is you. Do what you believe you must do. Be true to yourself, to your ideas and to your dreams.

16. Don't surrender leadership to the fracturing experiences of life. A brokenness can occur that leaves people without faith for the future. A young man said to me after his wife left him for another man, "I'm never going to trust another woman."

I said to him, "Believe in dreams. Never believe in hurts. Don't let your fracturing experience shape your future."

17. Don't surrender leadership to the flattening-out experiences of life. I have seen families that have withstood experiences that would crush others. Jean Van Allen learned that she had terminal cancer shortly after her husband Ed died in an airplane accident. She came back and did wonderful work at the church before she died. I asked her, "Where did you get the power to come back?" She said, "I thought, if I give up, two organizations will benefit, the mortuary and the cemetery. But if I hang in there for another month or so, my family will benefit. Maybe my church can benefit. Then I began to get inspired. I thought of hundreds of things I wanted to do. I just kept saying, 'I'm going to do this. I'm going to do this.'"

18. Do surrender leadership to one thing—faith. Let faith be in control of every decision you make and every action you take. Let the positive possibilities set your goals. When you look at your life and where it's headed, ask yourself these questions: "Who's in charge? Who's in control? To whom have I surrendered leadership?" Surrender leadership to faith. Surrender leadership to God. Let Him be in control of your life. Ask Him three questions: "God, who am I? Why am I here? Where am I headed?" His answers may surprise you. They will open your eyes to the beautiful person that you are and will become, as well as to the fantastic future that awaits you.

Robert Schuller is a best-selling author and preaches from the Crystal Cathedral.

17

Ten Natural Laws

by Hyrum W. Smith

Natural laws, like gravity, are fundamental patterns of nature and life. They describe things as they really are, as opposed to how we think they are or how we wish they were. Whether we agree with them or not, these laws ultimately govern our lives and operate independent of our awareness or wishes. Obeying them can help us gain control of our lives, improve our relationships, increase our personal productivity, and experience inner peace.

Law 1: You control your life by controlling your time. Controlling our lives means controlling our time, and controlling our time means controlling the events in our lives. You need to stop thinking "time management" and start thinking "event control." Too often we think time management has something to do with our watches. The only thing a watch tells you is how long it takes the sun to go across the sky. That's an event over which we have no control. The real issue is: What events can I control? Focusing on controlling the events of our lives makes all the difference.

Law 2: Your governing values are the foundation of personal success and fulfillment. Each of us lives according to a unique set of governing values. These values are the things that are most important to you. They are represented by the clearest answers you can give to these questions: What are the highest priorities in my life? and Of these priorities, which do I value most? Even though our governing values are our highest priorities, there often exists a gap between these ideals and our present realities.

Our performance relating to those values is never perfect. But as we improve, we bring together what we do and what we value.

Law 3: When your daily activities reflect your governing values, you experience inner peace. Once you identify your governing values, you must do something about them. Your values must find expression as measurable and achievable long-range and intermediate goals, which can then be translated into daily tasks that will move you toward their achievement. As you concentrate your time and energy on achieving tasks that have real meaning in your life, you become more productive and achieve inner peace—a sense of fulfillment and unity.

Law 4: To reach any significant goal, you must leave your comfort zone. External or physical comfort zones are easy to understand. But they are by no means the only type of comfort zones we have. Sometimes we develop mental, emotional, social, or psychological comfort zones. These can be much more difficult to leave than our physical comfort zones. Leaving our comfort zones requires effort and commitment.

Law 5: Daily planning leverages time through increased focus. Investing a little time in certain activities can free up time throughout the rest of the day. A daily planning session can act as a time lever. The cost is small—only 10 to 15 minutes a day—but you will enjoy many benefits all day long, such as clearly defined tasks with deadlines, increased focus on more important tasks, less time spent between projects, and a greater sense of accomplishment at the end of the day.

Law 6: Your behavior is a reflection of what you truly believe. All of us have had instances where we thought we believed something to be true, but in fact were doing nothing about it. What often happens is that we have another belief at work that is overriding or negating the belief we consciously know is true. If we can remove the deep-seated incorrect belief, then our behavior will start to come in line with the correct belief. In general, our behavior reflects what we really believe, and if our behavior doesn't reflect a consciously stated belief, we should take a careful look at our conflicting beliefs.

Law 7: You satisfy needs when your beliefs are in line with reality. How can you tell whether a belief, attitude, or opinion is correct? If the results of your behavior meet one or more of your basic needs, you probably have a correct belief. Conversely, if the results do not meet your needs, you can bet the belief in question is incorrect. If we can attack incorrect beliefs and destructive behaviors without attacking ourselves or others, we can solve most of the human relations and productivity problems we face.

Law 8: Negative behaviors are overcome by changing incorrect beliefs. Incorrect beliefs will produce negative, self-defeating behaviors. Left unchecked, negative behaviors will defeat your attempts to take control of your life. Any negative behavior is a symptom of a reactive way of life. Negative behavior is often the result of trying to meet needs with incorrect or inappropriate beliefs. Because the beliefs are not rooted in reality, they cannot produce behavior and results that will satisfy the unmet need. As we apply inappropriate behavior to satisfy the need, we get trapped in a downward spiral.

Law 9: Your self-esteem must ultimately come from within. We all seek to feel good about ourselves and validate our feelings of self-worth. But if we believe that our self-worth depends on the approval of others, we may act contrary to our deepest values. This can be a highly reactive way of living, and incredibly stressful. Only when we live in accordance with our own values will we find the self-esteem and fulfillment that come from within.

Law 10: Give more, and you'll have more. When we have an excess of anything—wealth, talent, knowledge, ability, experience—we have an obligation to share that excess with others in ways that make a difference. If we all shared in this way, most of the world's problems could be solved. When we find ways to share our excess with others—especially if they show through hard work, loyalty, creative talent, or even friendship that they deserve a portion of it—that excess will grow faster than if we hoard it for ourselves.

These 10 laws work. I know this from my own experience and from the experiences of thousands of others who have put them to the test.

Hyrum W. Smith is co-chairman of Franklin Covey Co., and is the author of *10 Natural Laws of Successful Time and Life Management* (Warner Books), from which this article is adapted and used with permission.

18

Work Leads to Success

by Harvey Mackay

recently read that Americans are working longer hours. Longer than who? Longer than our parents and grandparents? They worked 10- and 12-hour days, five and six days a week, to put food on the table and provide us education. Longer than senior executives and lawyers or doctors or top salespeople? Show me one of them who gets by on 40 hours per week.

If you aren't satisfied with average wages, then you may have to put out above-average effort. If you want some extra advantages for your family, the only surefire way I know to get them is to work. Hard. And sometimes that means part-time work in the kind of jobs that aren't posted in the Harvard Placement Office.

Hard work is not a bad thing. Sure, natural talent can make a big difference. But show me a "natural" hitter in baseball, and I'll show you someone who bangs the ball until his or her hands bleed to keep that stroke honed. Ask any surgeon about how much sleep he or she got for 10 years during medical school, internship, and residency. Ask any concert pianist how much practice it takes to perform a 40-minute concerto from memory. All these gigs take more than magic hands. Success takes iron determination and lots of hard work.

The harder you work, the luckier you'll get. For example, entrepreneur Ray Kroc sold milkshake machines. Kroc wanted to know why business was so good for one restaurant in San Bernardino, California, that it needed eight machines instead of two.

He learned that the McDonald brothers had changed the traditional drive-in format to attract families. It worked big time. Kroc bought them out and rolled out the concept nationwide, calling it McDonald's.

He later wrote down his philosophy: The world is full of talented failures, people who lack nothing in the way of education, intelligence, ability and charm, but who never seem to make it. The missing ingredient, the difference between success and failure, is determination, the will to press on.

Create a need only you can fill and don't quit until you do. Philip Pillsbury of the Pillsbury milling family had an international reputation as a connoisseur of fine foods and wines, but to the troops, his reputation as a man willing to do a hard, dirty job was the one that mattered.

A friend of mine told me about a fellow he works with—a Holocaust survivor, now in his late 70s, who was first captured by the Nazis when he was in his 20s. He escaped eight times. He finally made it to America with $5 in his pocket, no education, and no knowledge of English. He became a draftsman, then an architect. He is, by any standard, a financial success—and a living monument to the power of optimism.

You can always think of a reason to feel sorry for yourself. Don't fall for it. No one will care about your sad situation but you. And no one else will do much about it, either.

The opportunities you find in life invariably will come disguised as intolerable, impossible situations. You will find a thousand reasons why you cannot overcome them. Any one of those reasons will be sufficient to ensure your failure—if you allow it to happen. Don't. There is nothing, no handicap, no accident of birth or fate, no previous failure, no lack of resources so severe that it cannot be defeated.

Harvey Mackay is a businessman and a best-selling author of several books, including Swim With the Sharks Without Being Eaten Alive.

19

The Cycle of Success

by Roger Staubach

If *you're like me,* you want to be a success. Nothing feels better than to face a world of challenge and to triumph by finding the best within you.

The basic challenge is the same for you and me: to be as much as you can be. Get the most from the gifts you are given, and enjoy the fruits of a life well-lived. Success has no secrets. The main principles have been well known for years. But how often have you vowed to live more productively, more successfully—only to get swamped by daily demands?

Four Principles

Whatever your career, whatever your desires, three simple principles of success planning can help you sharpen your aim—and hit your target. They can help you learn what you want, and then link the life you live with the dreams you desire.

1. Set your goals. To get someplace, know where you're going. Goals put the dynamism of deliberate desire into all that you do. Take a few moments at the start of each day to write what you want to attain. Exactly. Specifically. Measurably. Goals help to marshal the strength of the mind for three reasons: goals increase focus, goals crystallize desires, and goals engage the imaginative power. The aim is to set specific, measurable goals.

2. Rank your priorities. To gain maximum success per minute invested, put first things first. Priorities keep your energy focused where payoff is greatest. Record your priorities—

those things needed to accomplish your goals—and then rank each task by priority: urgent, must do today; important, but could wait until tomorrow; useful, but no immediate hurry.

3. Act on urgent and important matters. Goals set the direction, but action brings the result. The simplest way to get the most from each moment is to do what's most important right then. The practical formula is to prioritize your activity—rank your tasks by order of importance—and follow through on those rankings in your daily action.

4. Assess your performance. To play at your best, keep score every day. A few seconds of self-assessment let you enjoy your achievements—and upgrade your performance. At the end of the day ask yourself: "Did I wind up where I aimed myself, or did I fizzle, get misdirected, or simply get swamped?" Regular self-assessment tightens the use of goals and priorities into a solid success system.

Rating Your Day

Rate your performance daily to assess how well you measure up to your goals.

• *On-goal rating.* Nothing is more important to success than to stay focused on your goals.

• *Alertness rating.* Success depends on alertness. If you feel dull and groggy, it's hard to do anything worthwhile. If you feel bright and alert, everything seems easy and enjoyable.

• *Achievement rating.* How many of your goals did you achieve? Either you achieve your goals or you don't. Were you right on goal with a high level of alertness? If you always do your best, goals will take care of themselves over time.

To get an accurate picture, you need to follow all three ratings, and adjust each of them in light of the others. It's a way to enliven the full range of success.

By merely putting your attention on each of these factors—On-Goal, Alertness, and Achievement—you tend to improve your performance.

Roger Staubach is chairman and CEO of the Staubach Company and former quarterback for the Dallas Cowboys.

20

Going the Distance

by George Sheehan

To *many people,* growing old seems like the end game in chess: life winding down in a series of small moves with lesser pieces. As I age I have discovered this is not true. I am not an elderly king stripped of my powers, reduced to a ragtail army of pawns. My life is not a defensive struggle of restricted options. Growing old is a game of verve and imagination and excitement. The outcome is not now a matter of strength, although that still remains, but of faith and courage, hope and wisdom. The aging game is a sport for which childhood and youth and maturity are no more than a preparation. Its scope comes as a surprise. It expands my life at a time when I expected it to diminish. It demands an excellence that no longer seemed necessary. It asks me to surpass what I did at the peak of my powers. Age will not accept second best.

In the aging game I must be all I ever was and am yet to be. What has gone before is no more than a learning period. A breaking in. Life, someone has said, is boot camp. If it is, age is the combat for which I was trained. Now I must take this person I have become and make each new day special. I must make good on the promise of every dawn I am privileged to see.

Life goes from a minor to a major key. The game builds to a climax. Every move assumes importance. One feels like a virtuoso. The gifts we have been given, the powers that empower us, the marvels that make us marvelous, are evident as never before. The truth is that we have lost nothing. The problem is not that

I am less than I was when I was young, it is that I am not more. It is past time to become my own person.

One also learns that honesty is the only policy. As I age I find less and less need to dissemble. I have little difficulty looking truth in the eye and admitting it. Lies and deception are time-consuming, and time becomes essential.

Time is what shapes the aging game. The clock and the calendar force me to make a move. Age does not permit the dallying with options that characterize youth. A labyrinth might be sport to the young. It brings panic to the old. My goal must be clear. The project outlined. The requirements understood. I must decide—if not this way, then there is no other way.

Fortunately, I find this commitment no problem. I accept the game and the goals I have developed in those formative years. I enjoy the self I have become. I no longer desire to be what I am not. My dissatisfaction is only in my failure to accomplish what is clearly attainable.

Such revelations frequently come late in life. They may arrive after decades of going in the wrong direction.

Why do I run?

We know that the effects of training are temporary. I cannot put fitness in the bank. If inactive, I will detrain in even less time than it took me to get in shape. I must be constantly in training. Otherwise the sedentary life will inexorably reduce my mental and emotional well-being.

So, I run each day to preserve the self I attained the day before. And coupled with this is the desire to secure the self yet to be. There can be no letup. If I do not run I will eventually lose all I have gained—and my future with it. However magnificent the achievement, without constant care the result is decay. There is nothing more brief than the laurel. Victory is of the moment. It must be followed by another victory and then another. I have to run just to stay in place.

Excellence is not something attained and put in a trophy case. It is not sought after, achieved and, thereafter, a steady state. It is a momentary phenomenon, a rare conjunction of body, mind, spirit at one's peak. Should I come to that peak I cannot stay there. I must start each day at the bottom and climb to the top. And then beyond that peak to another and yet another.

Through running I have learned what I can be and do. My body is now sensitive to the slightest change. It is particularly aware of any decline or decay. I can feel this lessening of the "me" that I have come to think of myself. Running has made this new me. Taken the raw material and honed it and delivered it back ready to do the work of a human being. I run so I do not lose the me I was yesterday and the me I might become tomorrow.

In 1985, I was in Dallas to give a talk at a fitness festival. The day before, I had challenged Dr. Ken Cooper's treadmill and had broken the record for my age group, 65 plus.

Afterward, as I lay on a table recovering, I felt as if I were joining the immortals. Despite my age, I had performed in the ninety-ninth percentile of the 70,000 tests done there.

Then Cooper announced he was going to give me a physical examination. Before I could protest, I was stripped down and experiencing what anyone experiences in a visit to the doctor. The results of this examination (which led to tests that would eventually discover a malignancy) made me face my own mortality.

Only a week before, I had been fretting about the normal vicissitudes of life—running, for one. My race times had deteriorated over the past year. I had rarely thought of my aging before; now I was becoming preoccupied with my age. I had reached a point where no amount of training made me improve. My writing was boring me. Many times before, I had thought that I was all written out. This time it was really true. When I took on a subject, I found I had done it before—and better. No phrases appeared that did not land with a thud and then lie there lifeless.

But I had known all these defeats in the past. The cycles came and went, as fundamental as the seasons and as unchangeable. I should have made up my mind to treat them as a fact of life, to accept that even champions have their slumps. The best of all know the worst of times—and use those experiences when the bright, beautiful, productive days return.

The news I received in Dallas gave me that different perspective. Even before the results of the test were in, my future had been decided. My life had been unalterably changed.

Psychologist Abraham Maslow called the years subsequent to his heart attack his "postmortem life." It was a time he viewed as a gift: hours of appreciating what he had taken for granted, days used in the best possible way.

The notion of a postmortem has even more implications. Postmortems are done to ascertain the cause of death. A postmortem life should uncover what was wrong with the previous one. How should I have lived that I would now be content? Why did I not bear my fruit, bring my message, reap my harvest? What became of the "I" that was to be? The questions multiply. One's life, which had previously seemed well ordered, is seen to be neither ordered nor well.

Each New Year's Day we think on these failures in the past. We make resolutions about the future. What has happened to me has made this traditional practice tremendously important. I see clearly that my life depends on what I decide to do with it.

So much of life passes without our being in it at all. For me, this is especially true about my relationships with other people. I have not entered their lives, nor they mine.

The big question is how one should live one's life. Writer and philosopher Miguel de Unamuno had this answer: "Our greatest endeavor must be to make ourselves irreplaceable—to make the fact that each one of us is unique and irreplaceable, that no one can fill the gap when we die, a practical truth."

After receiving my news, I learned I could do that—make that fact a practical truth. I will be irreplaceable. I will leave a gap. Each day, family and friends affirm my importance to them.

When you are between the sword and the stone, you know who you want standing beside you. When time is short, it becomes obvious who the essential people are in your life.

People who know they have cancer have a motto: "Make every day count." I have done that. What I have not done is make every person count. My life has been filled with the best of me. What it has not been filled with is the best of others.

I now know that Robert Frost was right. I have promises to keep, and miles to go before I sleep.

George Sheehan was a doctor, philosopher, record-setting marathoner, and author of *Going the Distance: One Man's Journey to the End of His Life* (Villard), from which this article is adapted.

21

What Makes for Success?

by Dave Thomas

T_here are all_ kinds of success and all kinds of ways to achieve it. I know bus drivers who are as successful as bankers. Success can take many forms, but one thing's for sure: Certain ingredients are necessary in any recipe for success, and they may be applied by anyone.

Success comes through doing the right things in developing proper skills, attitudes, and values. I have come to identify 10 "character traits" or "values" or "virtues." These are divided into four basic groups: 1) _Inward_—these have to do with getting your own act together successfully; 2) _Outward_—these are all about treating people right; 3) _Upward_—these are skills you need to know if you want to go beyond just doing an okay job and truly excel; and 4) _Onward_—these are attitudes you need to have in order to put yourself second and other people first.

Inward: Getting Your Own Act Together

Success starts inside. Unless your own attitude and beliefs are right, you can never be a success. That goes for being successful in raising your family or helping to lead your church or synagogue or just making a buck. People never have their acts together unless they are honest, they believe in something, and they develop basic discipline.

1. Honesty. Many good people may look at honesty backwards. They think that it's okay if they don't come forward with the whole truth until someone challenges them with the right questions. But honesty doesn't mean hiding in the weeds; it means stepping out and telling the whole truth. Honesty means being sincere. It also means being fair in all your dealings with others.

2. Faith. Honesty doesn't come from out of nowhere. It is a product of your moral convictions. But what do you do when your convictions are challenged? Faith gives you the strength to go on believing. Though I am a Christian, I respect the religions of others, and I think that they play a vital role in our society. But I don't support convictions or cults that are negative and lead only to hatred and fanaticism. Faith must be positive.

3. Discipline. Routine lies at the heart of discipline. Routine is what keeps us focused on the main things in life. But routine doesn't have to mean boring. Unless you have a strong, healthy routine, I doubt that you can live a successful life. Discipline means keeping things and people in their proper places.

Outward: Treating People Right

Success may start inside, but it doesn't mean anything until you draw other people into the picture. The key is whether you are fair to other folks—will you treat people right? If you are to treat people right, you have to master three fundamentals: caring, teamwork, and support. Caring is the rock that love is built upon. Caring is feeling what another person feels. Genuinely caring about people usually leads to success.

4. Teamwork. Teamwork is the starting point for treating people right. Most people think that teamwork is only important when competing against other teams. But competition is only part of the picture. In most areas, people have to work with rather than against each other to get something done. Win-win situations and partnerships are important results of teamwork. The best teams are ones that help people become better and achieve more than they ever thought they could on their own.

Upward: Going for Excellence

When you have your own act together and get along well with others, you're ready to reach for another goal, that of excellence. No one can excel in everything. In fact, excellence in any one little thing is hard enough. And don't forget: It's easy to become selfish when you "go for the gold." The graveyards of the world are loaded with people who lost it all at the same time they thought they were winning it all.

5. Motivation. Know what motivates you, and prove to yourself that this motivation is honest and worthwhile. But don't let too many different things motivate you, or you'll be tangled up in a maze of conflicts. Stay focused. Figure out what your motivations are going to be in the next step of your life before you arrive at it.

6. Creativity. Creativity means change, but if you don't use common sense when you change things around, you are likely to end up further behind than when you started. Not everybody can be creative. If you aren't creative yourself, your challenge is to learn how to work with people who are. And being creative doesn't always mean doing new things. Sometimes, it's using a creative idea that worked in one area and applying it to another.

7. Leadership. Everybody is saying that we need to stop putting leaders on pedestals. The real problem is finding leaders who truly deserve to keep their pedestals. What knocks off more leaders than anything else is failing to practice what they preach. Of all things leaders are supposed to do, nothing is more important than setting a good example. Ben Franklin had it right when he wrote in *Poor Richard's Almanac*, "Well done is better than well said." I don't think we should do away with pedestals; we ought to be putting more "little people" on them, people who have really achieved something, so that ordinary folks have a better, clearer idea of who's doing the job and who's setting the pace.

Onward: Putting Yourself Second and Others First

If going upward and reaching for excellence is where success gets tricky, going upward by putting yourself second and others first is where success gets tough. Most books on success tell you that you have "arrived" when you win the race. That's wrong. Truly successful people help others cross the finish line. People who make this last big step toward success have three things: responsibility, courage, and generation.

8. Responsibility. We try to teach children responsibility, but most of us don't learn the meaning of responsibility until we have gained solid experience, made some decisions, and learned from our mistakes—not the simple mistakes we make when "following orders" but mistakes we make when trying to do something hard or trying to excel. Making these mistakes teaches us judgment, and toughens our backbones. Mature responsibility means realizing that no single person can be responsible for everything. Responsible people refuse to take shortcuts, even though they are almost always available.

9. Courage. We tend to make courage too dramatic. Courage is often doing something simple, unpleasant, or boring again and again until we get it down pat. People who are physically challenged and who have the determination to get around their handicaps are great examples because their courage makes them test their limits every day in a way that the rest of us write off as small time or insignificant.

10. Generosity. A person who has modest means and won't share may be considered stingy. But rich people can give until they're purple and still not be truly generous. You have to give of yourself, not just of your wallet. I'm proud that so many Wendy's franchisees make significant donations to their communities, and they contribute leadership as well as dollars.

Added on to these ingredients are some others. Since I'm a hamburger cook, I call them "toppings." They are pickles and onions of how I look at success: Anything is possible within the laws of God and man. You can't cut corners on quality. When you help someone, you really help yourself. Pay attention to the basics. You can't make much progress walking forward if you don't keep your balance, and that means balance in every part of your life. Have a sense of urgency about most things you do, and you won't end up as the caboose. Focus on only one thing at a time, and on just a few things in a lifetime. Don't waste time trying to do things you know nothing about: Either learn the basics or steer clear. Remember that life is short and fragile. Live it as if you don't know if you are going to be around for the next breath. Don't take the people of our nation or their freedom for granted. Be yourself; don't take yourself too seriously. Do the right thing even when it may seem like the hardest thing in the world. Put more into life than you get out of it.

Dave Thomas is founder of Wendy's International and author of *Well Done: The Common Guy's Guide to Everyday Success.*

22

Struggle for Balance

by Ken Blanchard

New technology was supposed to make our lives easier and afford us more free time. The reality today is quite the opposite.

With fax machines, e-mail, cellular telephones, and pagers available to everyone, our lives are busier than ever. Not only do we not have more free time, we find it hard to get away from the demands of work. People can find us anywhere. Now we have phones on planes for making calls.

If you combine new technologies with the increasing rate of organizational change, the problem gets worse. We are working ourselves to death.

Stress levels have never been higher. When Norman Vincent Peale and I wrote *The Power of Ethical Management*, we agreed that each of us has two selves. We have an external task-oriented self and an internal reflective self. When the alarm goes off in the morning most of us jump to our feet into our external task-oriented selves. We're trying to get dressed while reading reports, we're on the phone in the car racing to a breakfast meeting, then we're busy all morning, then we rush to a luncheon meeting, then we're busy all afternoon. We end with a dinner meeting. Finally, when we get home, we fall into bed at 11:00 with barely enough strength to say goodnight to anybody who might be next to us. The next day we dive in all over again. One day leads to another, and we never take the time to awaken and experience our internal reflective selves, which is a longer, more deliberate process.

We repeat the same behavior on vacation. We're out of bed and onto the golf course, then tennis, then swimming. We race from one activity to another. Most people are exhausted when they return from vacation and have to come back home to rest.

My wife Margie has been teaching a successful seminar called "Strategies for Balancing Complicated Lives." She developed the program to help people reflect on their lives and see if they are going in the right direction. The focus is to help people gain a balance between success and fulfillment. We define fulfillment as connecting your life and work, connecting spiritually, and balancing time at work with your family and friends.

We once heard Rabbi Kushner, who wrote *When Bad Things Happen to Good People*, contend that there are two acts in life. Act 1 he called "Achieve," and Act 2, "Connect." Achieve is a very natural act for us. We are probably the only species that can set goals outside of survival. In today's world we behave like Achieve is the only thing that matters. Many people never get to Connect, which is all about fulfillment. Some people think right to the end that life is all about the next sale, the next buy. Yet on our deathbeds, we all wish we had loved more and taken more time for our family and friends. We help people develop their own mission statements, operating values, and life goals, and we give them a way to monitor the balance in their lives. They learn to separate out what was important from what was urgent and then focus their lives on making sure that important things get done—things like their relationships, their health, and their spirituality—to improve their quality of life.

What are you doing to look at your life to see if you are caught in a rat race? I have always loved Lily Tomlin's comment, "The problem with being in a rat race is even if you win, you're still a rat."

Ken Blanchard is chairman of Blanchard Training and Development, Inc., and coauthor of the *One Minute Manager* series.

23

Maximum Achievement

by Brian Tracy

Over *the years*, I have learned this: You can't hit a target you can't see. You can't accomplish wonderful things with your life if you have no idea of what they are. You must first become absolutely clear about what you want if you are serious about unlocking the extraordinary power that lies within you.

Every success I've enjoyed came after I had taken the time to think through what my goal would look like when it was accomplished.

You have to decide exactly what "success" means to you and what your life would look like if you made it into a masterpiece.

Seven Keys to Success

Seven ingredients of success are consistent with everything ever written on success and happiness. They characterize the lives and accomplishments of all high-performing men and women. By defining your success and happiness in terms of one or more of these seven ingredients, you create a clear target to aim at. You can then measure how well you're doing and where you need to make changes.

1. Peace of mind. Without peace of mind, nothing else has much value. You usually evaluate how well you are doing at any given time by how much inner peace you enjoy. You experience happiness and peace of mind whenever you are free from the destructive emotions of fear, anger, doubt, guilt, resentment and worry. In the absence of negative emotions, you enjoy peace of mind naturally, effortlessly. The key to happiness, then, is to eliminate, or minimize, what causes you negative stress, including negative people, situations and emotions that make you unhappy. Project forward in thought and imagine your ideal life. What combination of ingredients would have to exist for you to be perfectly happy? Don't worry about what's possible or not possible for you at the moment. Just define your life exactly as it would have to be for you to enjoy the peace of mind you desire.

What would you be doing? Where would you be living? Who would be there with you? How would you spend your time?

2. Health and energy. Just as peace of mind is your normal and natural mental state, experiencing health and energy is your normal and natural physical state. Your body has a natural bias toward health. It produces energy easily and in abundance in the absence of mental or physical interference. And radiant health exists in the absence of any pain, illness or disease. Wonderfully enough, your body is constructed in such a way that if you just stop doing certain things to it, it often recovers and becomes healthy and energetic all by itself.

If you achieve great things in the material world but lose your health or your peace of mind, you get little or no pleasure from your other accomplishments.

Imagine yourself enjoying perfect health. How would you feel? What would you weigh? What foods would you eat and what exercises would you do? What would you be doing more of, and less of?

3. Loving relationships. These are relationships with the people you love and care about, and the people who love and care about you. They are the real measure of how well you are doing. The fully functioning person has the ability to enter into and maintain long-term friendships and intimate relationships with other people. The very essence of your personality is demonstrated in the way you get along with others, and the way they get along with you.

At almost any time, you can measure how well you are doing in your relationships by one simple test: laughter. How much two people, or a family, laugh together is the surest single measure of how well things are going. When a relationship is truly happy, people laugh a lot when they're together. And when a relationship turns sour, the very first thing that goes is the laughter.

What is your ideal relationship? Who would it be with and what would it look like? If you could design your important relationships in every detail, what would you want more of, or less of? What could you do, starting today, to create these conditions in your life?

Without a clear idea of what you really want in a relationship with another person, you will probably find yourself in situations not of your own choosing. Problems in life are almost invariably "people problems." They come with hair on top, and talk back.

Only when you have your relationships under control and functioning harmoniously can you turn your thoughts toward the self-expression and self-actualization that enable you to fulfill your true potential.

4. Financial freedom. To be financially free means that you have enough money so that you don't worry about it continually. Achieving your own financial freedom is one of the most important goals and responsibilities of your life. It is far too important to be left to chance. Fully 80 percent of the population are preoccupied with money problems. This is not a happy, healthy way to live. Most worry, stress, anxiety and lost peace of mind are caused by money worries. Many health problems are caused by stress and worry about money. Many problems in relationships are caused by money worries, and one of the main causes for divorce is arguments over money. You owe it to yourself to develop your talents to the point where you know that you can earn enough money so that you don't have to worry about it.

What would your life look like if you achieved all your financial goals? What difference would it make in your activities? What would you be doing more of, or less of?

How much would you like to be earning one year, five years, ten years from today? What lifestyle would you like to be enjoying? How much would you like to have in the bank? How much would you like to be worth when you retire?

Most people never ask and answer these important questions in their entire lives! But if you can be perfectly clear about where you want to go financially, you can learn what you need to know and do to get there.

5. Worthy goals and ideals. Our deepest drive, according to Dr. Viktor E. Frankl, author of *Man's Search for Meaning*, is the need for meaning and purpose in life. To be truly happy, you need a clear sense of direction. You need a commitment to something bigger and more important than yourself. You need to feel that your life stands for something, that you are somehow making a valuable contribution. Happiness has been defined as "the progressive realization of a worthy ideal." You can only be happy when you are working step by step toward something that is important to you. What activities and accomplishments do you most enjoy? What were you doing in the past when you were the happiest? What sort of activities give you your greatest sense of meaning and purpose in life?

6. Self-knowledge and self-awareness. Self-knowledge goes hand in hand with inner happiness and outer achievement. To perform at your best, you need to know who you are and why you think and feel the way you do. You need to understand the forces and influences that have shaped your character from earliest childhood. You need to know why you react and respond the way you do to the people and situations around you. It is only when you understand and accept yourself that you can move forward in the other areas of your life.

7. Personal fulfillment. This is a feeling that you are becoming everything that you are capable of becoming. It is the sure knowledge that you are moving toward the realization of your full potential as a human being. You can learn how to achieve and maintain a positive, optimistic and cheerful mental attitude under almost all circumstances. You can learn how to develop a fully integrated, fully functioning, fully mature personality.

Defining the seven ingredients of success gives you a series of targets to aim at. When you define your life in ideal terms, when you have the courage to decide exactly what you want, you begin the process of unlocking your hidden powers to succeed.

Brian Tracy is a popular speaker and author of *Maximum Achievement.*

SECTION 3

Recovery

24

Bouncing Back

by Wally Amos

Personal **and** professional ruin once stared me in the face. But I managed to triumph over financial misfortune because I drew on the power within to turn a seemingly hopeless situation into an absolute winner.

I have learned that crises can turn out to be glorious benefits if we draw on universal wisdom to handle them. And problems, or challenges as I call them, are part of everyone's journey; they are valuable catalysts for our personal growth.

Each person is a jewel in a crown of unequaled beauty. I believe our imagination is the source of our individuality, our capacity for glory, and our own, peerless talents. I use the creative power of my mind to confront and shape my unique reality because I know that my vision involves me emotionally in my activities. I love and enjoy everything that I do, because I see my projects and experiences as an extension of myself. This total investment accounts for my success. Your own dreams and goals will become a reality to the extent that you pour yourself into them.

In meditation I let my imagination run rampant. Once I have dreamed my final goal, I construct mental pictures of the steps leading to the goal. Then I go out with a heart filled with passion and actualize what I have seen.

This technique of visualization has been used by many successful people. Andrew Carnegie began as an ordinary laborer in a steel mill, but managed to make himself a fortune. He used his imagination to dream, and then he went after it.

Everyone who has achieved greatness or fulfillment in life started out with a dream. Prayer and visualization call up your limitless spiritual resources to move you toward your vision. An unlimited power to create lies within you.

Motivate yourself toward your goal constantly, even when you appear to be failing. When I drop the ball while doing some small assignment, I still discover something important. Total commitment to your cause is like throwing a pebble into a lake; it creates ripples of value and good fortune throughout your life. Worthy results inevitably follow.

If you have boundless enthusiasm for the task at hand, you invigorate everyone around you and inspire them to take up the challenge even in difficult times. Your faith in the outcome will enable you to bounce back and generate support from others.

When you act according to your highest dreams, the outcome is often far grander than you might imagine. I moved to California with the dream of making it big in the entertainment industry, but I found myself going far beyond my first vision to a much greater enterprise. Outcomes are often not what I expect, yet I always find myself feeling completely satisfied with the way things work out.

When you have faith in the outcome, no matter what it may be, you cannot stop yourself from living and working with enthusiasm. As I put what I feel into action, I am filled with vitality and happiness. When you start out with an attitude like that, it enriches your life and mobilizes the people around you.

When I was forced out of my own company, it seemed utterly unfair. But while it looked like my brainchild had chosen to betray me, my intuition told me a divine plan was at work. I meditated, and reminded myself that life is a process and that everything works together for the best. I knew I was not a victim. Finally I came to a place of understanding which turned my heart right around. My suffering and rejection turned into a sense of comfort and peace.

This is what I learned: When things are not to your liking, like them as they are! When we are dissatisfied and depressed by our situation, or we are discontented because our circumstances are not what we think we want, we are standing in our own way. We must be in harmony with whatever happens in our lives if we wish to advance. Everything that comes to us is a gift, a stepping stone for us to reach our ideal. Whether it looks like a caress or a slap, if you maintain a positive mental attitude, it will contribute to your highest good.

When my company rejected me and gave me lemons, I decided to turn those lemons into lemonade. I remembered that doors had slammed in my face before, yet others had always opened to more brilliant prospects. I chose to see my current, seemingly adverse situation as the necessary impetus for creating a fabulous future. So I drew myself up and began to radiate a confident attitude.

This acceptance recharged me and became a powerful force in my ensuing renewal. I would not allow myself to see this event as defeat. I actually rejoiced in the knowledge that the opportunity to grow through this painful experience could be exciting! I might very well prosper by leaving the company; I could reach for new heights. I decided not to give up or complain about what had happened, or to give in to the ridiculous social notion that I was a failure. Rather I threw aside all the negative beliefs I had been taught in my life and I began to explore the possibilities ahead.

Conventional education does not teach us the truth that change is a positive force in our lives, and that it can act as a voyage of discovery from which great benefit may come.

10 Keys to Bouncing Back

I was once asked to outline the principles that helped me overcome my crisis. Here they are:

1. Don't become part of the problem. I was faced with an extremely unpleasant situation, but I did not internalize the dispute and defend myself in a combative manner. I let my attorney handle the legal details and I directed my attention towards starting Uncle Nonamé. I undertook to concentrate on the worthwhile things in my life and turned over the lawsuit to a trustworthy professional. In short, I focused on answers and solutions.

Reverend Robert Schuller speaks of the three fundamental ingredients for certain success: faith, focus, and follow-through. I like to add an extension to his idea: faith, focus, and follow-through equals fulfillment!

I am sure that if I did not have faith, the lawsuit would not have been resolved in my favor. Earl Nightingale once said that we become what we think about. So long as I believed in a positive outcome, victory was certain.

I focused on and identified my role in it all. I centered myself on it and decided how I could conduct myself in the most valuable manner. By concentrating on my purpose, I realized that developing Uncle Nonamé was my mission and I should do nothing else but work towards that. This provided the framework for me to move into my future.

I followed through by doing something for the Uncle Nonamé project every single day. Every morning I came up with something to get me just a little bit closer to achieving my goal. Fulfillment is a constant experience for me. There is an internal peace that comes from giving your all and looking at life from a positive angle.

2. Accept and acknowledge the reality of your situation. I realized that nothing could change the facts. Wishing the crisis away would not help. Getting angry and yelling would not help. Denying that this was a problem would make it worse. Taking it out on my loved ones would only add to my problems. I had to say to myself, "This is the way it is, and the course of events now depends entirely on me. I can turn this lemon into lemonade, or I can let it sour my whole life." I could only deal with my problem once I separated my emotions from the facts. Once I did that, I gained control of my situation and could make the necessary moves to resolve it.

3. Remain committed to creating a new life for yourself. Even through the darkest and most depressing times, even when I privately thought things could not be worse, I still woke up each morning determined to stay the course for as long as it lasted. I hardly had any choice. I had to redeem myself and take care of my family, so I had to keep my heart and my mind completely on track. I never gave up—I had to swim toward solutions or sink and lose everything.

4. Allow the experience to open you up to what you need to learn. Every situation is an education. I once had a habit of spending a lot of energy explaining myself and my course of action to other people. I was not wise or secure enough to hear their ideas. I guess I wanted to be right instead of happy. I learned through this lawsuit that if you open your mind to the voices of others, you will open your life to receiving your good. They say that there is a reason why God gave us two ears and one mouth—we should listen twice as much as we speak! I enhance my chances for growth and achievement as I learn to overcome my ego.

5. Maintain a positive mental attitude. A positive mental attitude is the basis of my philosophy of life. Positive people have positive effects on the world around them. W. Clement Stone says that the ultimate secret of success is to keep your mind on the things you want, and off the things that you do not want. It is as simple as that. Regardless of the appearance of a situation, there is always good to be found there. I make sure I seek out the beauty and wisdom in everything, and believe it or not, it is always there to be found.

6. Hold on to your faith. The noted Princeton professor Cornel West has an astute way of describing strong faith. He says, "Faith is stepping out onto nothing and landing on something." When we have faith, we reinforce our subconscious to make our lives move forward and flourish. We create our own circumstances, and our subconscious merely reproduces in our environment what we conjure up in our minds. Vitality, luck, love—everything comes to us as we draw such qualities out of ourselves.

7. Consciously practice living in the present. It always helps me to be mindful and aware of each moment so that I can make the best use of the time I have. If I had wasted my energy on thinking what could have gone wrong with the lawsuit, and how it could have turned out, I would have inhibited my ability to live each day effectively. If you live in the moment, you will realize that you have everything you need to deal with your life. The past cannot be changed nor the future predicted, but each moment in the present is a building block to creating a happy existence. I take care not to reflect on the past or project into the future—rather I believe it is the present that counts. "Do it now!" is my motto.

8. Keep your sense of enthusiasm alive and active. Enthusiasm creates joy. Joy creates more joy. Maintaining a joyful outlook and keeping a high level of enthusiasm can sometimes be difficult, but the more you do it, the easier it gets. The rewards always reflect what you invest.

9. Engage in acts of selflessness. Throughout the 19 months of the lawsuit, I still made time for my charitable and non-profit activities. Even if it is the last thing I am able to do, I will still devote myself to giving. I've been blessed with benefits both immeasurable and incredible. Not only did I receive emotional and spiritual support from my literacy and dropout prevention work, but I also ensured the success of my business by establishing myself in the heart of a community of people who came to my aid when I needed them.

10. Aim at responsibility, honesty, and integrity at all times. We are all part of the whole, and however we act determines what we receive. There is a law of cause and effect, and what we express comes back to us faithfully. I want the very best for myself, my family, society and this world. I realize that I can set my sights on that dream only if I am prepared to live my life in an honorable fashion with every action I take.

So I take care to follow these principles. I give the best of myself, and I get the best in return. Lemonade, anyone?

Wally Amos is the founder of the Famous Amos Cookie Company and the author of *Man With No Name*.

25

Women at Work

by Judy Woodruff

One of the first questions many young women ask me—and, encouragingly more and more men, too—is, "How hard is it to combine career and family?" I know from my own experience that family and career can be combined. At the same time, I know from experience that it is not easy.

I still laugh about that week when I broke up a trip to Ohio, where I was covering the president of the United States, to fly home for a fifth grade sleepover. I spent the night on the floor of a school gym, where we looked at the stars through a telescope, then I got up early the next morning, flew back to Ohio, and finished my reporting. I am lucky to have a great job. But I don't spend weekends thinking about Newt Gingrich or Bill Clinton or capital gains tax rates or even North Korea's nuclear capability. I worry about balancing soccer games and baseball practices with school picnics and sleepovers. Al Hunt, my husband, and I have three children, and there is one constant in our lives: we are always tired!

It's a tough, constant struggle. Almost every day, I worry—like most other mothers who work outside the home—whether I am striking the proper balance and what the long-lasting effects of my choice will be on my children. I feel guilty on those occasions when I miss a school play or a soccer game or get home too late to help with homework (our society's expectations of mothers have left a deep impression on me). But I believe I am a better mother and wife because I am fulfilled at work, and I know that I am a better journalist because of the joys of my family.

Like anything worthwhile, combining work and family requires real commitment. I often tell young people this: when you dream about the impressive goals you will achieve, dream just as hard about your family. And if you choose to become a full-time homemaker and caregiver, know what an honorable choice you have made.

We must remember that whatever choices women and men make, there are clear correlations between family structure and poverty, crime, and academic success. We must remember that parents today spend, overall, 40 percent less time with their children than parents did in 1965. Indeed, America at the end of the twentieth century is faced with a crisis of family. It is a crisis that affects every woman and man in this democracy because it tears at the fabric of the greatness of this country.

But while America remains the envy of the world in economics, higher education, and most other competitive barometers, it certainly is not the envy of the world in terms of family stability and sense of individual responsibility—the core relationships and values that define us as a people.

None of us can predict the future. But there always will be room for hard-working, creative people who very much want to make a contribution. What is most important is that each of us singles out the area she wants to contribute to, the needy spot in which to pour her passion, and works just as hard as she can in that area. You may barely make ends meet doing this But at the end of most days, you will feel fulfilled, feel that you are making a contribution, and you will not be consumed with worry about how much more you wish you were earning.

Each of us can try to make a difference in a child's life. We can take time to help a young, less fortunate child in a single-parent or nonparent home. We can spend just two hours a week with that boy or girl, only a little more than 1 percent of our time. Some of us may be able to do a lot more; all of us should be able to at least do this.

Judy Woodruff is senior correspondent and anchor at CNN. This article is taken from *A Voice of Our Own* (Jossey Bass).

26

The Bane of Busyness

by Eileen McDargh

The *mood of* many people is anything but upbeat. Cynicism, distrust and to-the-bone exhaustion are far more characteristic of employees in downsized corporations where the emphasis is placed on the mean side of lean. And, believe me, there is a difference between the leading edge and the bleeding edge.

What's a body to do? Let me offer some recommendations. Ask yourself, "Is my area being fruitful or merely productive?" Fruitful means bringing something efficiently to the market in such a fashion that we continue to bear quality fruit. It means not killing the tree in the process and that what we bring someone wants to buy. The term "merely productive" is best summarized in the words of Thoreau: "It's fine to be busy. So are the ants. What are you busy about?" I see a lot of busyness without fruitfulness. Remember the words of Peter Drucker, "Nothing is less productive than to make more efficient what should not be done at all."

All of us who work bear a responsibility for how we work. I know I find myself buying into the illusion that work must be completed before I rest. The only person who ever had his work done by Friday was Robinson Crusoe. We also accept tasks at face value and fail to understand three critical variables that can be negotiated so we're not overwhelmed: 1) *specifications*— what someone wants done; 2) *time*—how long the task will take; and 3) *resources*—what you need to get the task done (money, budget, people). Know which variable drives the assignment. Take time to understand exactly what the client or company really wants done. Don't be afraid to ask questions. How much leeway is included in the specifications? Ask about time: can the deadline be extended? Think creatively about resources—everything from temporary help to computers. Working harder is very different from working smarter.

A reflection for new eyes: A stitch in time only saves nine if what you're sewing fits you to begin with.

Eileen McDargh, author of *How to Work for a Living and Still Be Free to Live,* is a speaker, trainer and management consultant.

27

Balanced Success

by Zig Ziglar

Do *you normally* get more work done the day before you go on vacation than you generally get done in three or even four days? Chances are you do. So that begs the question: Why are you so much more productive that day?

What we do off the job determines how far we go on the job. Chances are superb that what you did off the job the day before vacation was simple: The night before, you invested a few minutes and made a list of what you must get done the next day. Then you prioritized that list and mentally said to yourself, "I must get this done tomorrow so that no one else has to do 'catch-up' work for me while I'm gone."

When you arrived the next day, you were very enthusiastic and optimistic. Throughout that day you focused on each task and disciplined yourself not to be distracted by outside influences. All of these activities made you the consummate team player as you realized that if you did what you were supposed to do the team would be able to function more effectively in your absence. You became infinitely more competent that day.

Since you would never permit anyone to take your bank book and write checks on your bank account, doesn't it make sense to treat every day like this one when you determined not to let anyone write checks on your time account?

I am encouraging you to work smarter. This approach will give you much greater job security. Can you imagine the boss firing anyone who performs every day like they perform the day before they go on vacation? However, despite your best efforts, the possibility is real that your company might still go out of business, downsize, merge or be taken over by another company—and there goes your job! If you perform every day like you perform the day before vacation and you still fall victim to circumstances beyond your control, would your employer write you a tremendous letter of recommendation? And doesn't that build employment security?

Suppose the impossible happens and the Dallas Cowboys go bankrupt. Owner Jerry Jones calls the players together, gives them the sad news and tells them they are now officially unemployed. Do you believe there's a good chance that Emmitt Smith, Troy Aikman, and Michael Irvin could find employment on other teams? Would these players get jobs with other teams because they once played for the Dallas Cowboys, or would they get jobs because of their ability, experience, commitment, and performance? Isn't it crystal clear that their employment security is in their hands—and your employment security is in your hands?

Your employment security has a direct bearing on your relationship with your family, so job performance has a direct bearing on balance in your life. If you were to come to work every day like you do the day before vacation, your effectiveness and leadership skills would grow so rapidly that you would either move up the ladder in the company or you would complete your assignments more quickly. Therefore, improved performance would enable you to get involved in personal growth and learning interpersonal relationships skills that would improve your chances of a balanced success.

What you do off the job impacts your effectiveness on the job, and what happens on the job affects your relationships at home. If you have a loving relationship with your mate, you take one attitude to work. If you have a "fight" at home, you take a different attitude to work. If you're severely reprimanded at work you take one attitude home with you; if you've been recognized, rewarded, and promoted on the job, you take an entirely different attitude back home.

Put Quality of Life First

If you seek standard of living (money) first, there's no guarantee that your quality of life is going to improve. However, if you put quality of life first, standard of living almost always goes up.

To be honest, I like the things money will buy—nice clothes, cars, and trips. At the same time, I love the things money will not buy. Money will buy me a house, but not a home; a bed, but not a good night's sleep; a companion, but not a friend; a good time, but not peace of mind.

I don't believe that everyone can be a multimillionaire, but I believe that you can be happier, healthier, more prosperous, more secure and have more friends, more peace of mind, better family relationships, and more hope.

You were born to win, but to be the winner you were born to be you must plan to win, prepare to win, and only then can you expect to win. To achieve a balanced success, your planning must include your personal, family, and business life. You've also got to set objectives in your physical, mental, and spiritual life. People who set specific goals and develop a plan of action to reach them tend to earn more money, be happier and healthier, and have better family relationships.

To achieve balanced success, take the "day-before-vacation" approach and apply the same principles and procedures at home. Spend time planning your next day on the job and planning your time with your family at home. That way, when you're on your job, you concentrate on the job, and when you're at home you really are at home.

When you plan things with your family, make the same commitment to follow through as you do on your job. A promise to take the family camping, to the zoo, on an outing or to a game is ultimately just as important to your success as integrity to your job. My commitment to give my family my time is just as important as my commitment to provide them with food, shelter and clothing.

When I'm home, I plan my family activities first because if I don't plan them, they either do not happen or end up being a hassle. Since making that decision, all phases of my life have been better. And since deciding to use Sunday as a day of worship, rest and family involvement, I've increased my productivity and creativity dramatically.

Zig Ziglar, author of *Over The Top*, is CEO of the Zig Ziglar Corporation.

28

Make the Connection

by Oprah Winfrey

One of my strongest memories is of being at a boxing match where Mike Tyson was fighting Tyrell Biggs. I remember hearing the announcer say, "In this corner, wearing black trunks, weighing 218 pounds, Mike Tyson." He was exactly the same weight I was. I thought, "I weigh as much as the heavyweight champion of the world." I left there determined once again to do something about my weight.

But it wasn't easy. During a four-year period, my goal was to get below 200 pounds. I tried every diet program imaginable. No matter what I did, I couldn't drop below 200. I would get as low as 208 and just stagnate. I'd start a workout program and be inconsistent, fail, and gain more weight.

When I was introduced to trainer Bob Greene, I thought, "He must be judging me. He must think, 'What a wallapalooza. I'm supposed to work with her?'" I know if I were him, that's what I would have been thinking. I couldn't look him in the eye.

I no longer had those thoughts after our first hike. Often while hiking, Bob and I would talk about why weight was such an issue for me. It was the first time anyone had explained why it had been so easy for me to gain the weight back after fasting. Having a physical explanation for it helped to ease my guilt. Low metabolism, no exercise = weight gain. Volumes of food, even low-fat food = weight gain.

In the weeks we worked together, I started to lose weight. But Bob didn't want me to weigh in. He wanted my goal to be moving toward a healthier lifestyle and not measuring my life in terms of weight. I started to feel lighter and better about myself.

All of the information about exercise, eating right, and how my body works helped me change the physical me. The most important part is to understand that it's not as much about the weight as it is about making the connection. That means looking after yourself every day and putting forth your best effort to love yourself enough to do what's best for you.

I have to say that's the greatest gift Bob Greene has given me. The biggest change I've made is a spiritual one. It comes from the realization that taking care of my body and my health is one of the greatest kinds of love I can give myself. Every day I put forth the effort to take care of myself. And there's no question I'm living a better life.

Only when you have self-awareness can you achieve self-acceptance. Only when you accept yourself can you experience self-love. And when you are capable of self-love, you learn to love. To express love is our ultimate goal. This is the path that leads you to the connection. And making the connection will change your life.

Know and Accept Yourself

Before you can make any physical changes, you need to know yourself. This is the foundation that will help you transform your life. Think of what happens when you build a house on a shaky foundation. It eventually crumbles. This is one of the reasons that so few individuals maintain their weight loss. If you don't know who you are or what you want, or you are unhappy with yourself, or you believe losing weight is the answer to all your problems, I can almost guarantee that the weight you lose will come back.

We all need to accept and love ourselves, no matter how we look. That means loving ourselves just as much now as when we reach our goal. Remember that food can be used as an anesthetic for dulling pain, but the original problem that caused you pain may remain unresolved. Not facing your problems now or along the way to your goal weight will only make it easier for you to lapse back into your old habits for dealing with pain.

Spend some time to know yourself, to understand your strengths and weaknesses, what motivates you, and what you like and dislike about yourself. Think about what you can and can't change about yourself, why you behave a certain way in a certain situation, and whether deep down inside you feel that you have control over your life or that you are a victim of circumstances. What do you want out of life? What are your spiritual beliefs? What makes you happy and sad?

Also, take a physical assessment of yourself. Stand in front of the mirror. The image you see reflects not just your eating and exercise habits. It reflects your life. And in life, nothing stays the same. Your body is no different. It's always changing, and you can make a decision to improve it or let it slide back.

People who are successful at losing weight permanently release all the external causes for being overweight. They accept responsibility for it themselves. After all, you and you alone are responsible for yourself. To blame people or events is a waste of time. It's easy to blame anything or anyone else for things that you don't like about yourself. But on the road to self-acceptance, this is a detour you can't afford to take.

Once you take responsibility for your life, it's time to move on to knowing what you really want regarding your body, mind, and soul.

Having tried a gajillion diets, I understand how when we want to lose weight, we tend to look for the answer outside ourselves. We want a magic solution—a secret formula. I used to wish somebody would just tell me the answer—show me the way. Someone did. But I've also learned what Glenda, the good witch, told Dorothy in *The Wizard of Oz*, "You always had it. You always had the power." The real secret is within you.

People often ask me what keeps me motivated to work out and eat right each day. I often jokingly respond, "I don't want my fat butt back." Although that's partially true, the real answer is that I never want to be anesthetized by the extra weight again. For me, overeating, not working out, and the inevitable weight gain that followed was my way of repressing, stifling emotions, procrastinating pain and discomfort, and avoiding my true feelings.

The truth is in spite of all my professional success, I now realize I've spent a lifetime being afraid. Afraid of not being liked. Afraid of hurting people's feelings. Afraid of confrontation. Afraid of being used. Afraid of expressing love.

True love begins with yourself. You can give and give and give to other people. Care for them, nurture them, support them. But it's the support and care and love you give yourself that gives you the real strength to care for and love others. This has been a difficult lesson for me to learn, but I'm finally getting it.

Each day, I put forth the effort to take care of myself, work out, eat healthy food, deal with my feelings and not bury them in a giant bag of Doritos, confront people when necessary, tell people the truth, and tell myself the truth. This has changed my life—I have been freed from my own personal prison.

I feel free—free to live in the moment. Free to enjoy everyone I can. When pain, betrayal, judgment or adversity come—I live that too. I can face it straight up and know that it, too, shall pass—every moment does. I'm no longer afraid. I am more connected to myself.

It's been a long time coming for me. This is not an easy journey to take. As a matter of fact, ridding yourself of the weight and all that the weight represents may be one of the most difficult things you can do. It can also be one of the most rewarding—it has been for me.

No doubt some of you are where I was three years ago. You've tried everything, failed many times over, and you think nothing will work. You have to change your perception. It's not about weight. It's about caring for yourself on a daily basis. Renew! Renew! Renew! Make the connection.

Oprah Winfrey, talk-show host, actress, philanthropist, and businesswoman, is the chairman of Harpo Entertainment Group in Chicago. She has been the host of the number-one talk show in the world for 11 years. She is the author of *Make the Connection* (Hyperion), from which this article is adapted.

29

The Maturity Challenge

by Leo Buscaglia

I *can't understand* why, given a choice between joy and despair, people often choose despair.

My daily experiences bring me into contact with individuals who seem almost lifeless and frighteningly apathetic. Most disturbing is their complete disrespect for their personhood. Most of them dislike themselves and where they are, and would choose, if they could, to be someone else and somewhere else. They are suspicious of others and guarded about their own selves, which they keep securely buried, even though they are painfully aware of the selves' presence. These people fear risks, lack faith, and scoff at hope as if it were romantic nonsense. They seem to prefer to live in constant anxiety, fear and regret. They are too frightened to live in the present and almost devastated by the past; too cynical to trust, and too suspicious to love. They mumble negative and bitter accusations and blame an uncaring God, neurotic parents or a sick society for placing them in a hopeless hell in which they feel helpless. They are either unaware of or unwilling to accept their potential, and take refuge in their limitations. Most of them kill time as if they had forever and never seem to seek other more viable solutions to their miserable situations.

Personal Responsibility

The responsibility for realizing our potential is ours. Our negligence to become fully functioning, no matter who we are or where we may be, will be potential forever lost. We are of value to the degree to which we are constantly actualizing as the unique persons we are at each moment of our lives.

Where do we start? We start at the present moment. We abandon the past and embrace the now. We start with the most valued possession and the only one that can lead us to our own full humanity—ourselves!

For me, living fully in each stage of life is the real challenge. It is apparent, for instance, that the love one learns in childhood has little relationship to that experienced by the mature person. So it is with dependence, loyalty, morality, and responsibility.

Each stage encompasses its own unique implications, requirements and potentials. These can only be actualized if each stage is lived and realized fully.

Mature persons have a sense of ego identity, a sense of who they are, separate and apart from others. But these separate persons also realize the need for both physical and psychological intimacy—a need to relate on a deep, meaningful level with others.

Mature persons have a sincere desire to be productive and to give of that productivity to others. They desire to create and share their creations. They accept their lives and work with satisfaction and joy. They put their talents into each endeavor and their imagination into recreating their lives each day. The mature artists of life are spontaneous, accepting, flexible, receptive to new experience, and suspicious of reality. They are harmonious with external forces but autonomous, busy with the processes of inventing their own lives. They see existence as a series of choices, the selection of which they must determine, and for which they are singularly responsible.

Mature persons have a deep spiritual sense in terms of their relationship with nature and other persons, and recognize the continual wonder of life and living. They make full use of their potentialities, accept themselves as part of the greater mystery of life, and share their love, joy and wisdom in an open, nonexploitative, responsible fashion.

Fully functioning, mature persons are continually growing, for they realize that maturity is not a goal, but rather a process; that the essence of maturity lies in creative and responsible choices. They have a flexible but nonconformist sense of identity, an accepting and vivid sense of who they are, what they can be and where their powers lie.

Fundamental to the mature person is the ability to form deep, intimate, meaningful relationships that are based upon an "unconditional regard" for the uniqueness of others. Mature people are affectionate, loving and sexually responsive; they are sociable, have friends and a sense of community. They are productive workers and dedicated to their labors. They embrace change for the improvement of themselves and others, as well as of the society in which they live. They are self-determined, inventive, good-humored, and comfortable in their world, with themselves and with others.

The Power Within

Each of us still has within us that which is necessary to remake the world. The principal motivational force necessary to accomplish this requires only our personal commitment to dedicate ourselves to the process of living our lives fully. Our lives are original documents which we alone can create. Either we create them or they will never exist.

The individual power is within each of us. It is ours to draw upon whenever we wish. It never dies. It simply lies dormant until we come to life. It is not mysterious. It is realized daily, each time we are fully aware and engaging enthusiastically and with abandon in the process of living.

Life is always ready and open at our side to share its resources. It simply awaits our embrace. It offers us our choices, approves our decisions and walks in our direction. It is continuously forgiving, amazingly adjustable, always accepting and forever encouraging. It is willing at any given moment to start afresh. It attempts always to guide us toward becoming our fully functioning and active selves, for in this way it can enhance itself. Only life, after all, begets life. There is nothing to fear. Hemingway said, "Man was not made for defeat." Armed with life on our side and a lifetime to experiment, the odds are in our favor.

Leo Buscaglia is a well-known author of many books, including *Personhood* (Fawcett/Columbine).

30

Without Clothes, We're All Naked

by Carla Perez

No *matter who* you are—regardless of your age, gender, race, nationality, or economic status—certain challenges confront you: to gain perspective and be at peace with childhood and family issues; to face each day without illusions about how life should be; to make choices and build for the future.

These tasks are not easy. You may have had a less-than-ideal childhood and unclear guidelines for adult living. In addition, you may not have a supportive extended family or long-term relationships with friends and neighbors. To lay your past to rest, you must face the situation directly. This includes serious soul-searching and draining old pockets of pain. As you heal, be warned: it can hurt—especially if your past involved neglect or abuse.

The Healing Process

The healing process has four steps.

- Gather information about your childhood from your own recollections and from memories of relatives and friends.
- Examine how as a child you responded to your family life and the ruts it has put you in as an adult.
- Let go of yesterday—the illusions and disappointments, the remorse and regrets, the ideal childhood you never had. I urge you to write letters to parents or other relatives to tap into the feelings and thoughts that continue to trouble you.
- Consider how your relatives might answer the letter if you were to send it.

Yesterday cannot be altered. Today can. And it will affect your tomorrows.

Accept What Is

While growing up, I harbored the fantasy that somehow I was special, and that fact would readily be apparent to everyone who met me. I shouldn't have to wait in line, fill out endless forms for taxes, passports, or job applications. And if I were upset or overwhelmed, other people would read my mind, drop whatever they were doing, and come to my rescue.

I was ill-prepared for life in the real lane: Day-to-day hurdles and occasional catastrophes occur; cars and appliances break down; relationships require time and energy; spouses and friends have their own agendas; children don't run like clockwork.

Though we are all exceptional in our own ways, there are no exceptions. To be adult means to stay in touch with who we are and where we are going; to feel our feelings and communicate our needs; to keep on top of clutter; to find meaningful work, affordable housing, friends, a loving mate; to decide who should put out the garbage; to accept losses related to jobs, youth, and health; and to maintain hope, perspective, and realistic expectations.

And that's not all! Old insecurities never die; bad things happen; emotionally limited individuals pop up everywhere; villains don't necessarily wear black; and when death steals loved ones, it's always too soon.

To give meaning to your days, deal with the *have-tos* and weed out unnecessary *shoulds*; grab an unexpected opportunity that comes your way. You can remember the past and plan for the future, but all you have is today.

On my morning walk, I pass by the corner fruit and vegetable store that offers mangos, four for a dollar. I buy 12. "Why so many?" asks my husband. "You can never have too many mangos," I reply. To me, mangos symbolize "la dolce vita." I love to eat one. Picks up the day. Gives it a bit of enjoyable decadence. I don't want to have too many days without mangos.

Carla Perez has been a practicing psychiatrist for 20 years and is the author of *Without Clothes, We're All Naked* (Impact).

31

From Panic to Power

by Lucinda Bassett

Everyone wants to feel confident. We all want to feel that we are strong, powerful, creative, and capable of greatness. We want to be in control of our lives and succeed in making our dreams come true. The truth is, we are and we can. Greatness is our birthright.

Just as greatness is a natural part of who we are, anxiety and fear are also a part of our lives. When we feel we are in control, we can keep our lives balanced and most everything runs smoothly. When we allow anxiety and fear to dominate, we start questioning our every move. The mere anticipation of these dreaded emotions can turn a potentially pleasant situation into a misery and a nightmare. When anxiety rules, your physical and emotional energy are drained to the point that everything is colored by worry and discomfort. Then your life becomes an endurance test rather than a celebration.

I lived much of my life controlled by a serious anxiety disorder. But now I consider my anxiety a gift. After suffering for years with fear and dread, I was forced to do something about it. Once my feelings of being out of control had escalated to where I felt that I could no longer function, I started looking for answers.

In my search for help, hope, and a better life, I found something wonderful—something that I didn't know was missing. I found that I am my own security. I didn't find it "out there." Instead, I found a powerful untapped source of strength and healing right inside myself. This wonderful sense of inner security has helped me through many difficult challenges. Now I understand that I am my own safe person and my own safe place. No matter what difficulties life brings, I can take care of me.

As a result of my struggles with anxiety and agoraphobia—fear of fearful feelings and thoughts often leading to avoidance behaviors—I have been blessed with my ability to help others who are suffering. Anxiety has no prejudices; it attacks everyone. It's a thief. It robs us of our present happiness by filling us with anticipatory worry. It makes us feel insecure and question our abilities. It makes us physically sick.

Whether we are suffering from severe anxiety or a less intense but underlying sense of discomfort and stress, we all have something in common. We want to feel better. We want to stop the vicious cycle of anxiety, fear, and worry. We want to feel relaxed, secure, in control, and at peace. We want to enjoy each day, to feel excited about our lives, to be willing and able to take risks, to do whatever we want to do without debilitating fear or anticipation.

You Hold the Key

Is that really possible? Absolutely. I suffered with anxiety and phobias all of my life. As a child, I had scary thoughts and bad dreams. My father's alcoholism created chaos and feelings of insecurity. As a teenager, I suffered from eating disorders and irritable bowel syndrome. I began avoiding situations where I couldn't come and go as I pleased, situations where I couldn't be in control.

By age 19, I was having panic attacks regularly. College was a challenge because it was difficult for me to sit in class. I felt anxious, panicky, and trapped. I made excuses for my lack of social activity and my inability to travel with friends. Riding in the back seat of cars and flying on planes was extremely difficult. My world became smaller and smaller.

By age 24, I was a top producer, selling advertising for a major radio station in Toledo, Ohio. In spite of my anxiety, I was doing well, but no one knew how I suffered. No one knew why I didn't ride in the car with my sales manager on sales calls, or why I couldn't sit in meetings with the doors closed. No one knew that I started every day with anticipation, fear, and dread.

If you feel anxious, fearful, overwhelmed, or stressed, I've been where you are. Now, I am completely recovered. Once I put an end to all the negativity, fear, and worry my anxiety created, I was able to use my time and energy in a positive way to do things even beyond my dreams.

Today I am living a full, exciting, happy, peaceful life. Is my life perfect? No. Do I still worry and have anxiety at times? Yes, but it's different. I used to worry endlessly about pointless things. Now, even when the issue is real and anxiety-producing, I control my reactions. You, too, can learn to control your thoughts, which in turn control your reactions. When you begin to trust yourself to try new things and take some risks, you will do things that you once only dreamed about.

You hold the key to getting your life back when you struggle with emotional challenges: You have the power to heal yourself. It's a matter of looking deep within for answers and insights. You might feel resistant at first. This is because you know you must change, and change can be scary. But look at your scared feelings as excitement. You are taking control by taking action.

Five Steps to Recovery

The process of going from panic to power is a gradual one. So, I suggest you do the following:

1. Begin by being compassionate, patient, and gentle with yourself. Stop thinking, saying, and doing things that make you feel bad, anxious, or upset with yourself.

2. Give yourself credit for any success. The simple act of buying this book shows that you are ready for change. Praise yourself for even the smallest accomplishments.

3. Keep an open mind. No matter who you are or what you've been through, I believe you can be helped. But you must want help. You must want to get better. You must want to take responsibility for yourself.

4. Don't overreact to your anxious feelings. Instead of fighting them, listen to them. Are you tired? Are you scaring yourself with your thoughts? Relax and let them pass.

5. Keep a journal. Note when you feel anxious; note when you feel good. Write down what you were doing, who you were with, what you just ate, and what time of day it was. This will help you see if there is a pattern to your anxious episodes. I think you will find that there is.

If you are someone who has been searching for answers, if you feel hopeless, please don't give up. Know you are not alone. There are answers. There is help. Don't worry that you are losing control. You're not. You just feel as if you are.

Life is a fabulous adventure. It wasn't meant to be lived in fear. Do you want to conquer fear? Is it your desire to go back to school or to start your own company? Perhaps you want to overcome a fear of public speaking or conquer a fear of flying. Or maybe you just want to stop your mind from racing with broken obsessive thoughts. You are full of possibilities. You are full of your own individual hopes and dreams, wishes and desires. You are more ready than ever to take control of your anxiety. Once you overcome your fears, it's all possible.

Lucinda Bassett, founder of the Midwest Center for Stress and Anxiety, is the author of *From Panic to Power*, from which this article is adapted and used with permission.

32

Power to Recover

by Betty Ford

You are empowered when you have the capability to control your personal agenda without being penalized. I am very proud that in my lifetime women have gained power and stature in almost every phase of life.

Part of our empowerment is the right to say no. To say no to harassment and unwanted sex—to say no to drugs or alcohol. And to have no understood as an honest answer and not open to interpretation. Another part of our empowerment is saying yes when we are in agreement! Our empowerment is feeling comfortable with our choices and secure with our decisions.

My husband's many years as a member of Congress, including 10 years as the minority leader in the House, and his service as vice president gave us comfortable footing for the stresses of being the first family. It was just not where we had planned to be at that point in our lives, and so it was a demanding time for all of us, but we were finding our way.

Two Big Blows

When I was diagnosed with breast cancer, I was dealt a terrible blow. But my breast cancer was detected early, and mastectomy and chemotherapy were successful in saving my life.

By being honest and outspoken in my position as first lady, I was able to change the public perception of breast cancer, to negate some old-fashioned attitudes about mastectomies, and to increase women's awareness of their need for screening for early detection.

Breast cancer was something that could be survived. And that survival taught me the value of living each day to the fullest. I learned not to project into the future but to embrace the wonders of today. I gained the special appreciation that comes when you are not sure how many more days you will be given.

These were important qualities to have when I confronted another health issue a few years later—specifically a dependence on prescription drugs and alcohol. On April 1, 1978, my family confronted me in what is known as an intervention. It was an action precipitated by the bonds of love. Love that was so strong it made my family want to do something to help me. Love enabled them to look beyond their own intense fear and denial and confront me with my own denial of my disease. My family came to the realization that they had to do something if I was to survive. I will be forever grateful that they had the courage and love to face me that day.

We have long lived with a stereotype of what a woman should be, what her role in her family and her community should be. A woman was a dutiful daughter, a loving wife, a devoted mother. She was put on a pedestal, and that pedestal required perfection. She was expected to go through the day untouched and unaffected by the troubles and turmoil of life because it was believed she was to be taken care of and protected by a man.

As an alcoholic, a woman did not meet the image. Somehow she had failed at achieving perfection. And no one wants to admit failure.

Until very recently, we women grew up receiving negative and confused messages about our roles and our capabilities. Many of us have lived our lives fulfilling the demands of what we should be rather than the reality of what we are. Being chemically dependent was certainly not included in those demands. So if we were alcoholic, we were quick to believe there was something very wrong and shameful about our lives. We brought these negative beliefs with us to treatment. Now, as more women seek treatment, this distorted vision of the "good woman" and "bad woman" is changing.

Road to Recovery

Fortunately for me, while I was in treatment I was helped by a special group of recovering women. They came to the hospital once a week and shared their feelings, their experiences, and their joy of recovery with me. Through this group of attractive, successful, and caring women, I began to accept myself not as an oddity but as a woman with a dependency on prescription drugs and alcohol.

When I left treatment, I knew I needed and wanted the support of other recovering women. Such support of others is an ongoing principle for anyone in recovery. I was told in treatment that my disease is "alcoholism," not "alcoholwasm." This disease is progressive, it is chronic, and it can be fatal. There is no cure, but it is one of the most treatable of all illnesses.

Awareness makes us all stronger. The more you know and understand, the more aware you are of the stigma every woman suffers when dealing with alcoholism, the better you will be able to encourage another woman when she reaches out for help.

As women, many of us have the added delights and pressures of being mothers and grandmothers. There are many ways in which we have the opportunity and the obligation to be positive, inspiring role models for the children in our lives. I think most of us realize that our youngsters look to us with bright, eager, unsophisticated eyes. They are anxious to copy us. The adult who tells a child not to drink and then drinks herself or himself is sending a very confusing message. The parent who says, "Thank goodness my kid doesn't do drugs; he only drinks beer," may feel that this level of alcoholic behavior is okay for a teenager. But for those under 21, beer is an illegal substance.

Beer and marijuana are considered gateway drugs for other more powerful drugs. Our children must learn that it isn't glamorous or fun to use drugs; it is dangerous and deadly. It is important both that we be role models for our children and that we show the young people in our lives how valued they are. The future is theirs, and they need to grow with a concept of their own worth, to know, absolutely, that they are extremely valuable to their families, to their friends, and to themselves.

Betty Ford was first lady of the United States from 1974 to 1977. This article was adapted from *A Voice of Our Own: Leading American Women Celebrate the Right to Vote*, edited by N.M. Neuman. (Jossey Bass).

SECTION 4
Life Values

33

Life Values

by William Bennett

T*he values by* which we live, and the values which we convey to our children, are our most important social issues.

Nothing more powerfully determines the shape of a child's life than his or her values, internal process, beliefs, sense of right and wrong. A child's values—more than his or her race, class, sex, ethnicity, neighborhood, genes, or background—will determine that child's fate. And it is given to families preeminently to provide those values.

Not all teachers are parents, but all parents are teachers—children's first teachers, children's all but indispensable teachers. And those parents should be able to send their children to schools that affirm the most deeply held convictions of parents.

Educators should not be allowed to usurp the authority from parents. The child is not a ward given to the state for its nurture. The child is a gift of God, given in trust to his or her parents. Our schools should treat our young people as gifts of God, not as subjects of social experimentation or as young animals in heat.

Fatherhood involves a lot more than getting a woman pregnant. Real fatherhood means love, commitment, sacrifice, and a willingness to share responsibility and not walk away from one's children. Young boys and girls who do not grow up with fathers are far more likely to drop out of school, to become promiscuous, to go on welfare, to use drugs, and to commit crime.

Marriage and parenthood should be held up, because in

marriage between husband and wife and in fatherhood and motherhood come blessings that cannot be won in any other way.

I believe the family to be our most important institution. In our time, efforts must be made to preserve and strengthen the family. Heroic efforts, if necessary. When I talk about traditional family values, I am not using code words, seeking a political wedge, or speaking to demean or to belittle others. I'm seeking to honor and to affirm what is best in us. I will never stop affirming that all real education is the architecture of the soul.

William Bennett is the former U.S. Secretary of Education. He is the best-selling author of *The Book of Virtues: A Treasury of Great Moral Stories.*

34

A Call to Action

by Hillary Rodham Clinton

Over the past 25 years, I have worked on issues relating to women, children, and families. And as first lady, I have learned even more about the challenges facing women. One challenge is to give voice to women whose experiences go unnoticed and whose words go unheard. Much of the work women do is not valued—not by economists, historians, or government leaders.

Those of us who have the opportunity to speak out have a responsibility to speak up for these women.

I want to speak up for women who are raising children on the minimum wage, women who can't afford health care or child care, women whose lives are threatened by violence, including violence in their own homes.

I want to speak up for women who are working all night as nurses, hotel clerks, and fast food chefs so that they can be at home during the day with their kids; and for women who simply don't have time to do everything they are called upon to do each day.

Most women work both inside and outside the home, usually by necessity. There is no formula for how women should lead their lives. We must respect the choices that each woman makes for herself and her family. Every woman deserves the chance to realize her God-given potential.

Both women and men are entitled to a range of personal security to the right to determine freely the number and spacing of the children they bear. No one should be forced to remain silent for fear of religious or political persecution, arrest, abuse, or torture.

Tragically, women are most often the ones whose human rights are violated. And when women are excluded from the political process, they become even more vulnerable to abuse.

I no longer find it acceptable to discuss women's rights as separate from human rights.

- It is a violation of human rights when babies are denied food, drowned, suffocated or have their spines broken simply because they are born girls.
- It is a violation of human rights when women and girls are sold into slavery or prostitution.
- It is a violation of human rights when women are doused with gasoline, set on fire, and burned to death because their marriage dowries are deemed too small.
- It is a violation of human rights when individual women are raped in their own communities and when thousands of women are subjected to rape as a tactic or prize of war.
- It is a violation of human rights when a leading cause of death worldwide among women ages fourteen to forty-four is the violence they are subjected to in their own homes by their own relatives.
- It is a violation of human rights when young girls are brutalized by the painful and degrading practice of genital mutilation.
- It is a violation of human rights when women are denied the right to plan their own families, and that includes being forced to have abortions or being sterilized against their will.

We must heed the call to action so that we can create a world in which every woman is treated with respect and dignity, every boy and girl is loved and cared for equally, and every family has the hope of a stable future.

Hillary Rodham Clinton is the first lady of the United States. This article was adapted from her speech to the United Nations Fourth World Conference in Beijing, China.

35

The Joy of Service

by Arnold Schwarzenegger

Today *everything is* in front of you—a whole new life with new goals and fresh dreams.

I remember the goal that I had about accomplishing the great American dream—of doing wonderful things in the movie business, becoming a great actor, a man who makes millions of dollars at the box office. I wanted to conquer Hollywood and the business world. I wanted to build real estate empires and restaurant chains.

I can tell you that on the way to achieving my dreams, moving up and turning those visions into reality, I had the most wonderful time, the most incredible experiences, and the greatest joys that you can imagine.

But, I can say that there is no joy like giving back to the community. I consider my biggest accomplishments to be those things I have done for the community. I love the feeling that I get each time I travel around the country promoting health and fitness for our youth. I also love going to the inner cities and inspiring kids to get off the streets and to get away from the violence and crime, and to say no to drugs, no to guns, no to gangs and say yes to education, yes to hope, yes to life. I love the feeling I have when I help the Special Olympians. My greatest joys come when I put time and effort back into the community.

A person's life is judged by how it touches the lives of others. It is what we leave behind, and how much positive effect we have and how much we help others, especially those who can't help themselves.

To have great joy, you must follow the philosophy of the strong helping the weak, the rich helping the poor, and the fortunate helping the less fortunate.

I have followed that philosophy, because I have been very blessed: I have been given much from God; I have been given much from this great nation; I have been given much from my parents, friends, and from other people who helped me get to the place where I am today.

I have learned that the right decision is one that helps and serves others. I want to quote the wonderful man who started the Peace Corps. He also happens to be my father-in-law, Sergeant Shriver. He said, "Serve, serve, serve. For in the end it is the servant who will save us all."

Arnold Schwarzenegger, a former Mr. Universe, is a well-known fitness enthusiast and actor.

36

Lessons in Life

by Barbara Bush

One night I got to thinking about what I have learned in life—sometimes the hard way—and the advice I'd like to give my precious children, if I could or would. I found myself at my computer composing a letter, which I never sent. But I would like to share it with you.

1. Try to find the good in people and forget the bad. Oh boy, I know how hard it is. Many years ago, I wasted so much time worrying about my mother. I suffered so because she and I had a "chemical thing." I loved her very much, but was hurt by her. (I am sure that I hurt her a lot, too.) Grace Walker said to me once, "Think of all the lovely things about your mother...all the things you love and are proud of about her." There were so many I couldn't count them all. I think that I expected her to be perfect. Nobody is perfect. Certainly not me. So look for the good in others.

2. Make friends, not enemies. Clara Barton, founder and president of the Red Cross, was once reminded of a wrong a friend had done to her years earlier. "Don't you remember?" the friend asked. "No," replied Clara firmly. "I distinctly remember forgetting that." Not bad advice. Isn't it better to make a friend than an enemy?

3. Don't talk about money to other people...either having it or not having it. It is embarrassing and quite vulgar.

4. Do not buy something that you cannot afford. You do not need it. If you really need something and can't afford it...for heaven's sake call home. That's what family is all about.

5. Do not try to live up to your neighbors. They won't look down on you if you don't have two television sets. They will look down on you if you buy things that you cannot afford. They are only interested in their possessions, not yours.

6. Be sure that you pay people back. If you have dinner at their house or they take you out, have them back. But remember, you don't need the expensive thing. You can make the best spaghetti in the world. People love to come to your home. Plan ahead, and it will be fun.

7. Value your friends. They are your most valuable asset. Remember, loyalty is a two-way street. It goes up and down. So be loyal to those people who are loyal to you. Your dad is the best example of two-way loyalty that I know.

8. Love your children. You are the best children any two people ever had. I know you will be as lucky. Your kids are great. Dad and I love them more than life itself. I think you know that about your dad. I do also. Remember what Robert Fulghum says: "Don't worry that your children never listen to you; worry that they are always watching you."

9. Enjoy life, for heaven's sake. Don't cry over things that were or things that aren't. Enjoy what you have now to the fullest. You really only have two choices: you can like what you do OR you can dislike it. I choose to like it, and what fun I have had. The other choice is no fun, and people do not want to be around a whiner. We can always find people who are worse off, and we don't have to look very far! Help them and forget yourself!

10. Above all, seek God. He will come to you if you look. Please set the example for your children. There is absolutely no down side to seeking God. George Bush and I have been the two luckiest people in the world, and when all the dust is settled and the crowds are gone, the things that matter are faith, family, and friends. And in this respect, we have been inordinately blessed.

Barbara Bush was the first lady of the U.S. from 1989 to 1993. She is the author of *Barbara Bush: A Memoir*, from which this article is adapted and used with permission.

37

Values Make Us Stronger

by Dan Quayle and Diane Medved

What is the secret to the long-term success of individuals and families? There is none. They simply practice the values that make people strong. These values aren't new or revolutionary; rather, they represent the foundation of any successful people.

Successful families share 10 things in common. They show by both word and example the importance of honesty, industry, morality, courage, respect, faith, compassion, humility, discipline, and duty.

1. Respect. A national devaluing of the virtue of respect began with the vicious tauntings in the late 1960s. Members of the "establishment" became the bad guys while dissident youth emerged as heroes. Since then, the "question-authority" mentality has eroded respect for the very men and women we should revere: scholars and elected officials, teachers and clergy, professionals and entrepreneurs. The best families don't permit a disrespectful attitude; instead, they pass along the importance of respect and honor.

2. Discipline. In the best families, discipline is a central theme of parenthood. Parents punish their children to reinforce the principle that certain behavior is not just inappropriate, it's not tolerated. For the most part, they approve of spanking a child for flagrant disobedience as a means of ensuring the child's well-being. However, they're apt to use spanking as a last resort after trying alternative disciplinary methods.

Children require limits, and parents are acting properly and lovingly when they spank their children with fair warning. It teaches them that "actions have consequences." Spanking is not seen by good parents as teaching violent responses to disliked behavior, a theory advanced by some prominent child experts. Rather, experience tells them it's a way to shape behavior toward respect and obedience, especially when firm discipline is balanced with great love.

3. Attentiveness. Open communication is a major family value, and a prerequisite to good communication is attentiveness. A common trait of effective parents is an intense interest in the moment-to-moment progress of each person in the family, especially the children. The parents observe their children for signs of distress, fatigue, illness, or other problems, as well as for indicators of success and happiness. They realize that each child is unique and has personal idiosyncrasies and requirements that demand differing responses.

4. Education. Strong families believe strongly in education as the key to advancement. There's great anxiety in America today about the deterioration of our educational system. Personal violence and mediocrity have become the norm. Given the level of these parents' involvement in their children's schooling, it's not surprising that all of their children attend college and continue to learn and advance their education beyond college.

5. Media curtailment. Strong families spend little time in front of the television. Nationwide, the average adult watches 26 hours of television and the average child 23 hours per week. In the best families, parents watch far fewer hours of television, and some don't bother with TV at all.

In fact, many parents like the idea of a TV-free home, despite the few "good" programs occasionally available. They seem to agree that no television show is as good for their children as reading a book, finishing homework, or playing outdoors. By minimizing time spent in nonparticipatory entertainment, especially TV, they spend more of their time communicating with their families instead of withdrawing from them.

6. Financial prudence. Regardless of their financial situation, effective parents emphasize to their children the virtues of thrift and frugality. The lesson universally conveyed to children in these healthy families is that nothing should be taken for granted. The value of money lies not in what it can buy but rather in what it took to make it. Money, in every case, is linked to work, and each family makes it clear that they owe everything they have to their work ethic. Children are given chores, not only as a normal contribution to the family but also to remind them that rewards come only from work.

7. *Self-sacrifice.* In the "Golden Age of Selfishness," from the late 1960s through the 1980s, a popular message was, "If it feels good, do it." If you don't like the confining vows of marriage, ignore them in favor of this new invention, "open marriage"; if you don't like requirements in college, agitate until they're relaxed. But in strong families, parents convey the notion that self-sacrifice not only benefits others but is personally rewarding as well. And while they may be self-sacrificial, they don't really see it that way. They're not "giving up" a personal desire in order to serve; they're doing their duty and gaining joy from their service to others. The families give and do and don't stop to consider what is "in it for them." They find happiness in giving of themselves.

8. *Commitment of faith.* Strong families are committed to their personal faiths. A *Newsweek* article notes that 57 percent of the population regularly attends church or religious services, and 80 percent of baby boomers consider themselves religious and believe in life after death. When parents display their own belief in God, children learn that a life based on faith provides a firm foundation. Parents are more credible when setting rules and goals if they can offer a grander scheme, a source of comfort, and a sense of the eternal. And children who see their parents submitting to God will be more willing to submit to their parents' rules as well.

9. *A sense of place.* Most strong families are deeply rooted in their communities. Others may change residences every other year, but these do not. Their communities form the bedrock of their lives, and their children return for holidays with their own children. Such stability helps make families and communities healthy. Children need to know that they are loved and supported. When the community they live in is interested in them, supports them, and encourages their successes, they will thrive.

10. Optimism and gratitude. "I love you; I appreciate you." While many people find it hard to say these words, healthy families are ever ready to recognize the good things in their lives. These families are grateful for life's blessings. The most needed value in America now is gratitude. There is so much to be grateful for: grateful to our Founding Fathers, to our families, to our friends and neighbors, and most of all, to God. America knows what family values are because so many Americans live them. Many families are still healthy and happy. Raising fine, achievement-oriented children is not a matter of obeying some obscure list of rules or following the lead of some strangers in Washington. It's a matter of doing what you think is right.

Whether you place your trust in scripture, history, science, reason, or common sense, all evidence suggests that strong families are the only earthly hope for the future of this or any other civilization. Try as we may to improve our society, our efforts will be in vain if we ever lose sight of that central truth. That means we can provide the best education in the world, but only if parents remember that they are the most important teachers of all. It means we can control crime, but only if our sons and daughters understand their responsibilities and their own worth as children of God. It means we can reverse the cycle of dependency, but only if our homes are places of discipline, self-respect, and hope. In the words of Michael Novak: "If things go well with the family, life is worth living; when the family falters, life falls apart." Preserve, protect, and defend the family: This is the first order of business for our civilization and our political system.

Dan Quayle is former Vice President of the United States of America. Diane Medved is an author. This article is adapted from *The American Family: Discovering the Values That Make Us Strong.*

38

Faith in Action

by Lady Margaret Thatcher

America is the only country founded on liberty. The Founding Fathers journeyed to America across perilous seas not for subsidies, not to make a fortune even, but to worship God in their own way—and to perpetuate freedom and justice more widely.

They believed in the sanctity of the individual: that each person matters equally, and that each of us is accountable to our God for our actions and for the use of our talents.

It was that faith, that courage, that infused the life of this new nation destined to become uniquely great. It's a most remarkable story of faith in action, and it changed the world.

Of course, there can be no freedom or liberty without a rule of law, because otherwise it would be the freedom of the strong to oppress the weak.

Expediency and pragmatism are never enough. When I had to pull Britain around, we worked out our principles, once again renewed them, worked out our policies from our principles, and then implemented our programs. And they were all of a piece because we had the faith on our side, and we knew that what we were doing was fundamentally right.

Not only are pragmatism and expediency not enough, but fellowship isn't enough either. If you are going to chart the way into a better future, you must have a compass of enduring values and principles.

Those of us who believe passionately in a free society should put the case of capitalism much more positively than it merely "performs better." Capitalism is economic liberty. It is a vital element in the network of freedom. It is a moral quality, for it reflects the right of people to use their God-given talents.

You get the best results by men and women exercising their God-given talents and working together and responding to the needs of the market in a community of work. The market requires a framework of law, but these laws must never stifle the spirit of enterprise.

Beware dependency on the state. Once used to such support, people are never satisfied to have it otherwise. Don't shrink from looking after your neighbor as yourself. It's part of your creed.

Freedom has its responsibilities. As we look ahead, some people are taking the freedom and leaving the responsibilities. The values and virtues we prize are honesty, self-discipline, a sense of responsibility to one's family, a sense of loyalty to one's employer and staff, and pride in the quality of one's work.

These qualities are threatened by a lack of respect for the rights, freedom, property, and thought of others. This manifests itself in two ways: 1) in rising crime and violence, as people go and take what they want and have no sense of morality toward others; and 2) in the breakdown of the family, arising from vastly more children born to single parents.

No government can afford the police necessary to assure our safety unless the overwhelming majority of us are guided by an inner, personal code of morality. And you will not get that code unless children are brought up in a family that gives them the affection they seek, that makes them feel they belong, and that guides them to the future. The greatest inequality today is not inequality of wealth or income. It is the inequality between the child brought up in a loving, supportive family and one who has been denied that birthright.

Lady Margaret Thatcher served as prime minister of Great Britain from 1979–90.

39

Challenge of Change

by Rosalynn Carter

Many people do good things in their lives that aren't publicly applauded.

My mother is one example. When I was 13, my father died. I was the oldest of four children; my little sister was only four years old. We were still grieving my father when, less than one year later, my mother's mother died.

My mother had always been secure and dependent. An only child of doting parents, she married my father who was nine years older and always provided and cared for her. Suddenly she found herself alone with four small children to raise.

She did what she had to do; she went to work. She raised us, sending us all to college, which had been my father's wish. She took care of her widowed father until he died at age 95. A successful mother, daughter, and postal clerk, she was an achiever.

I didn't notice how my mother must have felt then, but what she taught me by her example affected my later actions.

I was very young when Jimmy Carter and I married. He was in the Navy and was frequently away during the first two years of our marriage. I had to take care of everything. At the end of the first year, I had a baby. I felt overwhelmed, but Jimmy assumed that I could manage well and always made me feel that he was proud of me. I was forced to discover that I could do things I never thought I could do, developing in the process a real feeling of independence.

These experiences helped prepare me to accept whatever position I found myself in and to do the best I could with it, whether as the bride of a naval officer, as the wife of a peanut farmer, as a real business partner, or as first lady of Georgia.

Jimmy was governor of Georgia for 10 years. There were new experiences every day and new things to learn. Learning, as Georgia's first lady, to make speeches, which I did out of sheer determination; learning not to be so concerned about criticism (which was good preparation for the White House), nor to be so intimidated by celebrities; learning that I could make a difference by pursuing the issues I thought were important and tapping the people who could help me most; daring to help Jimmy run for president; and finally, serving our country as first lady. In all of these experiences, I found that there are different ways to learn and meet challenges.

In the Governor's Mansion and in the White House, I had a chance to work on issues important to women, to work with the mentally afflicted, the elderly, the physically handicapped, the children in inner cities. I learned early that a first lady has influence, and I tried not to waste the opportunities I had.

In thinking about my mother's life and my life, I'm struck with how much the role of women has changed. Just look at my daughter, Amy, and the opportunities she has. She can do almost anything she wants to do, become a leader in almost any field.

But her generation is also faced with the challenge of figuring out how to take advantage of these opportunities and still make those contributions to family and community that have always fallen to women: being good mothers, good wives, good neighbors and good leaders. Young women today have a lot of pressure on them that women never had before. As a result, men are having to recognize the value of what traditionally has been the woman's role and share in the responsibilities.

We are living at a wonderful time, and our future is bright; but it still depends on how well we meet the challenges that face us. It will take the talents, contributions, and leadership of every one of us to achieve the quality of life all of us want for ourselves and for the generations that come after us.

Rosalynn Carter is a former first lady of the United States. This article was adapted from *A Voice of Our Own: Leading American Women Celebrate the Right to Vote* (Jossey Bass).

40

Three Words

by Martha Saunders

I *have found three* three-word phrases useful in my life. These three phrases include:

First, "I'll be there." Have you ever thought about what a balm those three words can create? If you've ever had to call for a plumber over a weekend you know how really good these words can feel. Or if you've been stranded on the road with car trouble and have used your last quarter to call a friend, you know how good those words can be.

Recently I was talking with a local businessperson who occasionally hires our graduates, and she told me the single most impressive thing a job candidate can do is to demonstrate a real interest in the well-being of that business. Someone who will help further the objectives of that organization, whether or not he or she is "on the clock," is going to be a valuable person. In other words, be somebody who will be there.

Elizabeth, the Queen Mother of England, was once asked whether the little princesses (Elizabeth and Margaret Rose) would leave England after the Blitz of 1940. The queen replied: "The children will not leave England unless I do. I shall not leave unless their father does, and the king will not leave the country in any circumstances whatever." In other words, "I'll be there."

Second, "Maybe you're right." Think about it. If more people were to learn to say "maybe you're right," the marriage counselors would be out of business and, with a little luck, the gun shops as well. I know from experience it can have a disarming effect on an opponent in an argument.

When we get so hung up on getting our own way that we will not concede on any point, we are doing ourselves a real disservice.

Third, "Your heart knows." When I was a little girl, whenever I was faced with a hard decision I would turn to my caregiver and ask, "What should I do?" Her response was always the same: "Your heart knows."

"My heart knows?" I would think to myself. "What's that supposed to mean?" I would ask. "I need advice here. I need you to tell me what to do."

She would just smile and say, "Your heart knows, honey."

But as I was an imperious child, I would put my hand on my hip and say, "Maybe so, but my heart isn't talking!"

To this she would respond, "Learn to listen."

Life doesn't come in the form of a degree plan. There's no Great Advisor out there who will give you a checklist and say, "Do these things and you'll succeed."

To some extent, the page is blank now. You may have a rough outline of where you're headed, but I can assure you, you won't get there without having to make some tough decisions—and decision making is never easy.

You may find people to suggest what you should do, but for the most part, no one will be willing to accept the responsibility for your mistakes. You'll have to make your own choices.

So, learn to listen to your heart. The psychologists call this "turning to our subconscious." Spiritual leaders call it "turning to a higher power." Whatever you call it, you can find the right answers for your life. It's a powerful gift that all the education or degrees in the world can't acquire for you. You've had it all along—now, you're going to have to use it. "The difficulty in life is choosing." Choose well.

Martha Saunders is the Associate Dean of the College of Liberal Arts and Sciences at the University of West Florida. This article was adapted from her speech to graduates.

41

My Pyramid of Success

by John Wooden

My *father had* a profound influence on my life. Both my philosophy of life and coaching came largely from him. Even as a small boy I always had great respect for him because I knew he would always be fair with me and had my best interests at heart. And I soon learned that if my dad couldn't say something good about another person, he wouldn't say anything at all.

A truly gentle man, Dad read the Bible daily; he wanted us to read it, and we did. That is why I keep a copy on my desk today. It's not a decoration. It is well marked and read. The fact that I never heard Dad swear surely accounts for the fact that even today when I get mad, I can only say "goodness gracious, sakes alive."

I remember so well what Dad gave me for graduation from our little country grade school in Centerton, Indiana. It was a piece of paper on which he had written a creed that he suggested I try to live by. It read:

Be true to yourself. Make each day your masterpiece. Help others. Drink deeply from good books, especially the Bible. Make friendship a fine art. Build a shelter against a rainy day. Pray for guidance. Count and give thanks for your blessings every day.

I carried Dad's handwritten original of that in my wallet for many years until it wore out. Then I had copies made. I keep one in my wallet today along with another quote that further exemplifies my father's spirit:

Four things a man must learn to do
If he would make his life more true:
To think without confusion more clearly,
To love his fellow-man sincerely,
To act from honest motives purely,
To trust in God and heaven securely.

I can't say that I have always lived by that creed, but I have tried. My dad did love his fellow-man sincerely. He was honest to the nth degree and had a great trust and faith in the Lord. And he taught us many lessons in integrity and honesty which we never forgot. Even though he was never able financially to help his sons through college, he is undoubtedly responsible for the fact that all of us graduated from college, got advanced degrees, and entered the teaching profession.

On the farm, Dad always made sure we had some fun mixed with our work. I was eight years old when Dad made a basket for us out of an old tomato basket with the bottom knocked out. He nailed it up on a wall at one end of the hayloft in the barn. Our basketball was made out of old rags stuffed inside a pair of my mother's black cotton hose. She would sew it up, by hand, into a round form. It's hard to imagine now, but we were able to dribble that thing.

Then Dad forged a ring out of iron for a basket. That iron ring was pretty close to regulation. It went up in the loft, and we made sure we used hay from that end first so we could play basketball.

Early in life, my father convinced me that the only road to success was through education. I was always a fairly good student, and I have Mom and Dad to thank for that. They encouraged us to read, to study, and to learn. My lifelong interest in poetry comes from my father. He read poetry every night, either before or after reading the Bible. Frequently, he read aloud to all of us. These are some of the happiest memories of my childhood.

My Pyramid of Success

Over the years, I developed what is now known as my Pyramid of Success. Only one person can judge your success—you. You can fool everyone else, but in the final analysis, only you know whether you took the shortcut, the easy way out, or cheated. No one else does. I know that I look back with regret on some things that seemed to be success to others.

No building is better than its structural foundation, and no man is better than his mental foundation. Therefore, my original cornerstones are still the same—industriousness and enthusiasm. There is no substitute for work. And to really work hard at something you must enjoy it. If you're not enthusiastic, you can't work up to your maximum ability.

The three attributes that I place between the cornerstones are friendship, cooperation, and loyalty. They illustrate that it takes united effort to tie in the cornerstones.

The anchor blocks of the second tier of the pyramid are self-control and intentness. If you lose self-control everything will fall. You cannot function physically or mentally or in any other way unless your emotions are under control. That's why I prefer my team to maintain a constant, slightly increasing level of achievement, rather than hitting a number of peaks. I believe that there is a corresponding valley for every peak, just as there is a disappointment for every joy. The important thing is that we recognize the good things and not get lost in self-pity over misfortunes. To perform properly, you must be intent. There has to be a definite purpose and goal if you are to progress. If you are not intent about what you are doing, you won't resist the temptation to do something else that might be more fun at the moment.

Alertness and initiative are in the second tier. You've got to be constantly alive and alert and looking for ways to improve. In basketball, you must be alert to take advantage of an opponent's error or weakness. Coupled with this must be the individual initiative to act alone. You must have the courage to make decisions.

Now, at the heart of the pyramid is condition. I stressed conditioning with my players, not only physical conditioning but also moral, mental, and spiritual conditioning. I always told my players that our team condition depended on two factors—how hard they worked on the floor during practice and how well they behaved between practices. You can neither attain nor maintain proper condition without working at both.

At the very center—the heart of the structure—is skill. Skill is the ability to execute the fundamentals quickly and precisely at the right time.

Team spirit is also an important block in the heart of the structure. This is an eagerness to sacrifice personal glory for the welfare of the group as a whole. It's togetherness and consideration for others. If players are not considerate of one another, there is no way we can have the proper team play that is needed. It is not necessary for everyone to particularly like each other to play well together, but they must respect each other and subordinate selfishness to the welfare of the team. The team must come first.

Poise and confidence will come from condition, skill, and team spirit. To have poise and be truly confident you must be in condition, know you are fundamentally sound, and possess the proper team attitude. You must be prepared and know that you are prepared.

Near the pinnacle must be competitive greatness. And this cannot be attained without poise and confidence.

This pyramid is tied together with other qualities. You tie them together with ambition, which if properly focused can be a tremendous asset, but if it is out of focus, it can be a detriment. You must be adaptable to work with others and to meet the challenge of different situations. And you must display resourcefulness because in almost every situation good judgment is necessary.

Fight gives you the ability to do it and not be afraid of a tough battle. Faith must walk beside fight because it is essential that you believe in your objective, and you can't have faith without prayer. Patience must be strong because the road will be rough at times and you should not expect too much too soon. Then come reliability, integrity, honesty, and sincerity.

All of these tie the blocks together into a solid structure. When all these factors are united, you can build toward a success that is based on your own personal set of goals, not those of someone else.

John Wooden is the retired basketball coach of UCLA and Indiana State University. This article was adapted from his book *They Call Me Coach,* written with Jack Tobih (Contemporary Books).

42

Cynicism or Faith?

by Al Gore

In a time of social fragmentation, vulgarity often becomes a way of life. To be shocking becomes more important—and often more profitable—than to be civil or creative or truly original. Given the degree of vulgarity in our society, cynicism seems almost irresistible. Sometimes it even looks like a refuge of sanity, a rational response to a world seemingly driven by the fast hustle, the pseudo-event, the rage for sensationalism.

But cynicism represents a secession from society, a dissolution of the bonds between people and families and communities, an indifference to the fate of anything beyond the self.

Cynicism is deadly. It bites everything it can reach—like a dog with a foot caught in a trap. And then it devours itself. It drains us of the will to improve; it diminishes our public spirit; it saps our inventiveness; it withers our souls. Cynics often see themselves as merely being world-weary. There is no new thing under the sun, the cynics say. They claim that their weariness is wisdom. But it is usually merely posturing. Their weariness seems to be most effective when they consider the aspirations of those beneath them, who have neither power nor influence nor wealth. For these unfortunates, nothing can be done, the cynics declare.

Hope is considered an affront to rationality; the notion that the individual has a responsibility for the community is considered a dangerous radicalism. And those who toil in quiet places and for little reward to lift up the fallen, to comfort the afflicted, and to protect the weak are regarded as fools.

Ultimately, however, the life of a cynic is lonely and self-destructive. It is our human nature to make connections with other human beings. The gift of sympathy for one another is one of the most powerful sentiments we ever feel. If we do not have it, we are not human. Indeed it is so powerful that the cynic who denies it goes to war with himself.

A few years ago, Shelby Steele wrote about his pain as a child, when he was mistreated by a teacher who called him stupid. He said that the teacher's declaration created a terrible reality for him. If the teacher told him he was stupid, he thought he must be stupid. He wrote:

I mention this experience as an example of how one's innate capacity for insecurity is expanded and deepened, of how a disbelieving part of the self is brought to life and forever joined to the believing self. As children we are all wounded in some way and to some degree by the wild world we encounter. From these wounds a disbelieving anti-self is born, an internal antagonist and saboteur that embraces the world's negative view of us, that believes our wounds are justified by our own unworthiness, and that entrenches itself as a lifelong voice of doubt.

Search for Healing

Where, then, do we search for healing? What is our strategy for reconciliation with our future and where is our vision for sustainable hope?

I have come to believe that our healing can be found in our relationships with one another and in a shared commitment to higher purposes in the face of adversity.

A personal event that fundamentally changed the way I viewed the world was an accident that almost killed our son. I will not repeat the story here, except to say that the most important lesson for me was that people I didn't even know reached out to me and to my family. They lifted us up in their hearts and in their prayers with compassion of such intensity that I felt it as a palpable force, a healing reaching out of those multitudes of caring souls and falling on us like a mantle of divine grace.

Since then, I have dwelled on our connections to one another and on the fact that as human beings, we are astonishingly similar in the most important parts of our existence.

I don't know what barriers in my soul had prevented me from understanding emotionally that basic connection to others until after they reached out to me in the dark of my family's sorrow. But I suppose it was a form of cynicism on my part. If cynicism is based on alienation and fragmentation, I believe that the brokenness that separates the cynic from others is the outward sign of an inner division between the head and the heart. This isolation of intellect from feelings and emotions is the essence of the cynic condition. For the cynic, feelings are easily separated from behavior.

Having felt their power in my own life, I believe that sympathy and compassion are revolutionary forces in the world at large and that they are working now. I have come to believe in hope over despair, striving over resignation, faith over cynicism.

I believe in the power of knowledge to make the world a better place. Cynics may say: People have never learned anything from history. But the cynics are wrong: we have the capacity to learn from our mistakes and transcend our past. Indeed, truth—Veritas—can set us free.

I believe in finding fulfillment in family, for the family is the true center of a meaningful life. Cynics may say: All families are confining and ultimately dysfunctional. The very idea of family is outdated and unworkable. But the cynics are wrong: it is in our families that we learn to love.

I believe in serving God and trying to understand and obey God's will for our lives. Cynics may wave the idea away, saying God is a myth, useful in providing comfort to the ignorant and in keeping them obedient. I know in my heart—beyond all arguing and beyond any doubt—that the cynics are wrong.

In the end, we face a fundamental choice: cynicism or faith. Each is equally capable of taking root in our souls and shaping our lives as self-fulfilling prophecies. We must open our hearts to one another and build on all creative possibilities. I believe in our future.

Al Gore is the Vice President of the United States of America. This article is adapted from *Vital Speeches.*

SECTION 5

Ongoing Growth

43

The Art of Self-Motivation

by Bonnie St. John Deane

Growing up in hospitals, in leg braces, and on the wrong side of the tracks didn't stop me from believing that an African-American girl with only one leg could learn to ski. And as soon as I learned to ski a little, I set my sights on qualifying to compete in the 1984 Disabled Olympics in Innsbruck, Austria.

Such a big dream, such an outrageous dream, made me stand taller just thinking about it.

My big break came when an elite ski academy in Vermont accepted me as a student. For three months I searched for grants, scholarships, and sponsors to no avail. I will never forget the moment when I told the headmaster I couldn't afford the tuition and I had failed to find sponsors. He said, "Come anyway." I knew this opportunity would change my life.

And then it happened. On the first day of school at Burke Mountain Academy, I broke my leg—my real leg—while playing on a skateboard.

As the only kid there with one leg, I had so badly wanted to show them I could run obstacle courses, jump rope, and play soccer. Instead, walking on crutches with my artificial leg I could barely get from my room to dinner without tripping on stones in the path. Being so thoroughly inept among a crowd of super athletes hurt more than my injuries. At night I cried in my pillow to keep my roommate from hearing.

Although the doctor removed my cast after six weeks, my luck did not improve. Less than a week out of the cast, my artificial leg broke in half. When you think things can't get any worse, you're wrong. For three weeks my prosthesis roamed the country, lost in the U.S. Postal Service.

Years later, standing on the winner's platform in Innsbruck, Austria, as the silver medal was hung around my neck, I could hear the national anthem playing and see the Stars and Stripes fluttering behind me in the frosty night air. Dreams of that moment had pulled me through all the tough times.

Do you have a powerful dream that captures your heart and picks you up when you fall down?

Who or what motivates you? When I am asked that question, I must answer, "I motivate me."

Five Exercises

The easiest, most reliable system for motivating yourself is to put yourself annually through five exercises that take less than one hour to complete.

You can learn to take conscious control of your motivation by measuring it with the Motivation Meter System. For any project or goal you are working on, you can increase your motivation by: 1) finding bigger payoffs; 2) improving your odds of success; and 3) reducing the work required.

Exercise 1: What are your payoffs? Payoffs are more than money. Money payoffs represent the means to things like expensive cars or bigger houses. Nonmonetary rewards, like a job you love or more time with family, can also be payoffs. In all cases, "things" are less important than what those things mean to you personally. Payoffs are highly individual. "The only vision that motivates you is your vision," says William O'Brien, president of Hanover Insurance. Making personal payoffs bigger doesn't necessarily entail getting more things or setting higher goals. Bigger payoffs are those that have more meaning for you.

Spend five minutes listing everything you have ever wanted to have in your life: new clothes, vacations, ideal relationships, peak experiences, career accomplishments, and so on. Circle an item on the list which you never actually get around to doing anything about. Look at the list of dreams you made in Exercise 1. Star items that excite you. Using the dream you circled (the one you never do anything about), complete Exercise 2.

Exercise 2: Find the deeper meaning in your goals. For each goal or dream, ask yourself, "What's in it for me? Why do I want it?" Dig underneath your goals to find personally compelling reasons. Dig down to find out what you want out of life. Like a little child, keep asking yourself why. If the final answer is, "I should," or "My boss wants me to," scratch it off your list.

If you can't scratch the goal or dream off your list but it doesn't excite you, change it. Expand it. Aim higher. When digging underneath your dream uncovers meaningless results, aim higher. "Be bold," wrote Basil King, "and mighty forces will come to your aid." Norman Vincent Peale urged, "Learn to pray big prayers. Prayers have to have suction in them."

Exercise 3: Get your dreams at half price! Who wouldn't be more motivated to go after his or her dreams if less work was involved? Learn to cut the work required for your goals in half by using at least one of these seven creative ways to cut the work: 1) Find ways to reach two different goals with one piece of work; 2) Do the hard work (preparation and research); 3) Work immediately. Get started and don't wait until you have all the answers. Just do things that fit your schedule, things on the way to something else; 4) Work fun. Don't insist on doing it your way; encourage people to work with their skills, personalities, and styles; 5) Work together—get an exercise buddy, start a support group, or join a professional association; 6) Work lovingly; and 7) Work effectively. Do what you love, and love what you do.

Exercise 4: Stop underestimating your odds for success. Do you frequently underestimate your chances for success? Underestimating your odds can stop you dead in your tracks; overestimating your odds for success can spur you to tackle monumental tasks...and win! Entrepreneurs tend to be overly optimistic. Err on the side of optimism.

To dramatically improve your motivation: spend less time around negative people, smile at people even when they are rude, spend more time around a successful or upbeat person, read or listen to motivational material, enroll in a health club or start an exercise program, sign up for a workshop on self-esteem, confidence, positive thinking, or public speaking.

But don't ever settle for "positive thinking" techniques alone. Personally, positive thinking won't motivate me unless I also investigate the real odds and work on improving them.

Exercise 5: Change your real odds of winning. Put the odds in your favor; learn from people who have done what you want to do. List your resources. Circle one and act on it. Don't feel you have to do everything at once. You can get there with books, people or groups. Do what you love!

This Motivation Meter System can help you achieve anything that your mind can conceive. My story, for example, doesn't end on the winner's platform at the Olympics. Since then, I have motivated myself to finish degrees from Harvard and Oxford, to win a Rhodes scholarship, to win awards as an IBM sales representative, and to garner high praise as a White House official on the national Economic Council. Truly, there is no limit.

Bonnie St. John Deane has won olympic ski medals and is the author of *The Winning Spirit.*

44

A Responsible Life

by Nathaniel Branden

We *are responsible* for our lives, well-being, and actions in all areas open to our choice. I find that we may operate self-responsibly in one context and passively in another. For example, we may be self-responsible financially but dependent emotionally. We may be proactive when working for ourselves but reactive and non-accountable when working for someone else. We may take a good deal of responsibility for our physical health while taking none for the effects of our irrational behavior with our children or spouse.

I propose that we need to be self-responsible in each of the following 10 categories:

1. I am responsible for the level of consciousness I bring to my activities. When I am working on a project, listening to a lecture, playing with my child, talking with my spouse, deliberating whether to have another drink, reading my performance review, wrestling with a personal problem, driving my car, I am responsible for the level of consciousness I bring to the occasion.

2. I am responsible for my choices, decisions, and actions. I am the cause of my choices, decisions, and actions. It is I who chooses, decides, and acts. If I do so knowing my responsibility, I am more likely to proceed wisely and appropriately than if I make myself oblivious of my role as source. If I accept responsibility, I am far more likely to choose, decide, and act in ways that will not later cause embarrassment, shame, or regret.

3. I am responsible for the fulfillment of my desires. One common cause of frustration and unhappiness is people's fantasy of a rescuer who will someday materialize to solve their problems and fulfill their wishes. This is why I always stress that no one is coming. No one is coming to save me; no one is coming to make life right for me; no one is coming to solve my problems. If I don't do something, nothing is going to get better. The great advantage of fully accepting this is that it puts power back in our own hands. We are through with waiting and free to act. As long as I am overempowering others, imagining only someone else can save me, I am disempowering myself. In my avoidance of self-responsibility, I condemn myself to passivity and helplessness.

4. I am responsible for my beliefs and my values. The responsible individual strives to make beliefs and values conscious so that they can be critically scrutinized and so that he or she can be more in control. It does not take much probing to discover that much of the time we are merely reflecting what others believe and value. Or else our ideas seem to be born out of our feelings and "instincts." We are comfortable only with people whose feelings are like our own and uncomfortable with those whose feelings aren't.

5. I am responsible for how I prioritize my time. Our choices and decisions determine whether the disposition of our time and energy reflects our professed values or is incongruent with them. If we are clear in our understanding that how we prioritize time is our choice and our responsibility, then we are more likely to address and correct the contradictions than if we tell ourselves that we are somehow victims of circumstances. Taking responsibility is the key to finding a solution.

6. I am responsible for my choice of companions. Naturally many of us find it tempting to avoid this kind of responsibility. The advantage is that then we do not have to take action. We can suffer, feel sorry for ourselves, and blame others. And we can fulfill a subconscious life script that tells us pain is our destiny. The disadvantage is that then we are stuck in our unhappiness, defeated and disempowered, all our power granted to anyone but ourselves. Yet the power is there, waiting to be taken. The price is to recognize and own our choices.

7. I am responsible for how I deal with people. Whatever I choose to say or do, I am the author of my behavior. I am responsible for how I speak and how I listen. I am responsible for the rationality or irrationality of my dealings with others. I am responsible for the respect or disrespect I bring to encounters, for the fairness or unfairness, the kindness or unkindness, the generosity or meanness. Whether I choose to speak to others' intelligence, or to pander to their vices, it is my choice. Whether I keep my promises or break them, it is my decision.

8. I am responsible for what I do about my feelings and emotions. If we are educated to understand, or manage to learn on our own, that we are responsible for the actions we take on the basis of our feelings, the chances are that we will be less impulsive and more thoughtful about our behavior. But if we operate on the implicit premise that whatever impulse hits us must be followed, if we believe that feelings are to be obeyed without judgment, then we become reckless drivers through our existence.

9. I am responsible for my happiness. If I take the position that my happiness is primarily in my own hands, I give myself enormous power. I am not waiting for events or other people to make me happy. I am not trapped by blame, alibis, or self-pity. I am free to look at the options available in any situation and respond in the wisest way I can. If something is wrong, my response is not, "Someone's got to do something!" but "What can I do? What possibilities exist? What needs to be done?"

10. I am responsible for my life and well-being. In taking responsibility for our own existence, we implicitly recognize that other human beings are not our servants and do not exist for other human beings as means to our ends, just as we are not means to their ends. We are not entitled to demand that others work and live for our sake, just as we do not work and live for theirs. We are each of us ends in ourselves. Morally and rationally, we are obliged to respect one another's right to self-interest.

My observations are not meant to argue against mutual aid or social cooperation. There are many good reasons for people to choose to help one another in times of difficulty—voluntarily. But one is not born with a "right" to the mind, work, and energy of others. Any one of us may need help from strangers at some point in our lives, but self-responsible people do not demand it as their due. They appreciate it as an act of generosity. They do not imagine they were born holding a mortgage on the energy and assets of other people, although plenty of politicians and intellectuals tell them otherwise.

Today the attitude of entitlement has reached epidemic proportions. A *Time* magazine journalist noted: "If I want it, I need it. If I need, it, I have a right to it. If I have a right to it, someone owes it to me. Or else I'll sue." This short statement condenses the antithesis or self-responsibility.

The idea of living self-responsibly has many applications, from carrying one's weight in a marriage to acknowledging authorship of one's actions to earning one's living.

Nathaniel Branden, Ph.D., is a practicing clinician in Los Angeles and a best-selling author. This article was adapted from his most recent book, *Taking Responsibility*.

45

Mr. Peak Performance

An Interview with
Charles Garfield

W*hat would you say to any person who wants to launch a personal development program?*

I would tell them to start by paying attention to their own bodies—to their exercise, fitness, and food habits and patterns—because my experience suggests that the base of all discipline, improvement and progression is the body. Freud made the comment that "biology is destiny." That comment translates in a number of ways, but he once said that we are all limited by the body and that our capacity for transformation is based in the body. I believe that the limitations of our bodies are not negatives, but we always have to pay homage to the body.

What research have you done to support your belief in the importance of overall body fitness?

My early research determined the difference between peak performers and workaholics. I found that the peak performers have better than average health and relationships on the job and at home, and that workaholics have poorer than average health and relationships on the job and at home. And when I looked into what peak performers do to maintain health, I invariably found that they had some systematic form of physical exercise, recreation, and relaxation that was integrated into their lives, not something they did two weeks a year on vacation, but something that was much more integrated into their lives. When your body is functioning at a high level, it's inextricably linked to your success elsewhere—emotionally, spiritually, productively.

On a personal level, how has the condition of your body correlated with your performance in other areas?

My body weight can vary up to 30 pounds. I don't like that, but I can use weight as an indicator of what else is going right or wrong in my life. So when I start adding a few pounds, I start paying attention to what that means in other areas. Getting back into top shape seems to turn my life around, my productivity, my capability to reach new levels.

There is high interest in Daniel Goleman's idea of "emotional intelligence." Your work suggests a bigger idea—whole-body intelligence.

I believe that emotions are indicators of the body condition. For example, anybody who drinks too much coffee knows that emotionally you find yourself overreacting to things that normally wouldn't upset you. Why is that? It's because the body's responsiveness is heightened.

In many ways, our intelligence about how we are personally is often based on body clues. For example, most people register tension somewhere in the body. If you are able, first, to see tension as an indicator of what I call "psycho-social stress," stress in your environment and in your life, then your body can serve you extremely well as an indicator of what's going on in your life.

If you ignore powerful indicators of stress for long periods of time, you become a candidate for coronary heart disease. So many men—and increasingly more women—bear tremendous physical demands and elevated levels of stress. Their bodies warn them for years before they have any big trouble. Then the body has to act in dramatic ways—such as a heart attack—to get their attention.

Why do so many otherwise intelligent people mistreat their bodies?

One answer is that food becomes a major source of gratification at a level it never was intended to be. Food is about nourishment. You're supposed to eat what you need to live, not as an additional source of life gratification.

There are several ways to mistreat your body, but obesity is certainly one of them. A major factor leading to obesity is the fact that people are not being gratified in other ways on the job and at home.

Another reason for obesity, of course, is that we don't exercise enough. We don't use the knowledge that we have. We are inundated with great information on how to stay fit. It isn't a mystery. It's just that we're not applying what we already know. Strange, isn't it, especially in the context of wanting to perform well and move ahead. It's well-documented that there's a correlation between your fitness and not only your performance but also basic things like self-esteem, self-love, self-acceptance. And, the old idea about the body being a temple of the mind is still true—and so it moves into the spiritual realm. If you hope to love another, you've got to learn to love yourself, and one basic expression of self-love is taking care of your physical body.

Is there also a strong correlation between fitness and social relationships?

The basic desires we all have for health, happiness, and joy seem to be all tied to the body, and also to social relationships. It's all one piece; it's all tied together. How you're doing physically, your level of fitness, how you feel about yourself from a physical point of view will affect self-esteem. Your self-esteem is a primary indicator of how successful you'll be in your relationships. If you do not feel attractive to other people, you'll probably feel ill at ease. I have a friend who is very bright but severely overweight, and his obesity makes him tremendously sensitive, self-conscious, and uncomfortable in social situations.

So, mind, body, and spirit are all interconnected?

Yes, and that's why the maintenance habit is so important. I work out five days a week, because I believe that maintenance of my body carries over into my relationships. If you abuse your own body, you will likely carry that abuse into your relationships because you lose the basic truth that things have to be maintained.

To the extent that you don't feel good about your body, to the extent that you're angry at yourself, you will either internalize that and feel passively worse about yourself and have low self-esteem, or you will project it outward onto other people. You will project anger when really it's anger toward yourself. You will be inappropriately angry at the other people.

The best ways to undermine your career and your productivity are to ruin your health and ruin your relationships.

Charles Garfield is CEO of the Charles Garfield Group and author of *Second to None* and *Peak Performers.*

46

The Taming of the Ego

by Wayne Dyer

I *once asked* Abraham Maslow, "What do you mean when you say self-actualization?" He said, "There are just two things to remember: one is to learn to become independent of the good opinion of other people, and the second is to master the art of being detached from the fruits of your labors."

For example, you may experience turbulence in your life. But you can learn how to remove yourself from the turbulence and see that it's just your body going through it.

When you become the observer, you detach yourself from the outcome. You get your ego and everything in the material world out of the picture, and you allow the highest part of you to observe the circumstance. You remove all that inner turbulence, anguish, fear, and anxiety, and you then replace it with the calmness of a detached observer. The minute you sense that calmness, the solution is at hand. You're not operating from adrenaline or fear or angst.

When you face a crisis or deadline from the perspective that you only have so much time and "have to hurry," you become one more person who brings stress and anxiety to the problem.

It's in the taming of the ego that you find the sacred in your life. You find greater strength when you can stop being so focused on you and your bottom line and start reaching out to others.

They said of Jesus and Buddha that when they went into a village, their very presence raised the consciousness of those around them. They radiated a blissful serenity. That kind of peace is where you can resolve virtually any difficulty.

One of the great teachers in my life was Carl Jung. He died when I was four years old, but he wrote a book called *Modern Man in Search of a Soul* wherein he talked about four stages that people go through to reach maturity.

The highest stage is the stage of the Spirit. This is when you finally recognize that you are not an athlete, a warrior, or a statesman, that you are in this world, but not of this world. You recognize that you are not a human being having a spiritual experience, but you are a spiritual being having a human experience. In a sense, this life is all very temporary; this life is like a garage where we park our souls for a time, but our inner spirits are not so confined. The mystery of that is what we call unconditional love. When you are able to live this unconditional love you will have achieved this final state.

It doesn't happen if you try to figure it out using logic or look for results in the material world. When you start taking your attention off of building your business so you can make more money—and instead put your attention on serving everyone who comes through your door as best you can—your energy begins to spread...and the more people become attracted to your office.

That energy becomes infectious, because it promotes more of that love—and as it does, your bottom line becomes blacker and blacker. But your awareness is always focused on serving. You let the bottom line take care of itself.

It has worked for me in my organization. My profits, my sales, my bookings have just gone up and up over the years, and I have less and less concern with how I am doing.

So, Lighten Up

You do not have to strive to prove anything—unless, of course, you choose to listen to your omnipresent false self, which stipulates that if you don't stay busy pursuing something you are a failure.

It can be difficult to lighten up and understand that life is what happens while you are making other plans. Each and every instant of your life takes place in the present moment.

Using your present moments to chase after future moments is an ego-based activity. Your ego wants you to feel incomplete so that it can control your life. Your false self would keep you in perpetual motion chasing after more and more until your final breath.

Your higher self does not want you to be lazy or without purpose but to realize the power in knowing that this moment is your entire life. When you stop focusing on past or future moments, you release the stress and tension that accompany the striving lifestyle. With that release, you become more productive and peaceful than you are when you look behind or ahead of yourself and don't allow your mind to rest in the still center or the present moment.

Contrary to what your ego attempts to convince you, you will not simply vegetate, become homeless or an irresponsible drifter when you stop striving. What will happen is that you will lighten up and become so engrossed in your mission that you are more vibrant. With this power, you will discover that you are free to serve whatever you are intuitively drawn to.

When you stop striving and start knowing that you are on a divine mission, and that you are not alone, you will be guided to the experience of arriving. That experience will introduce you to the bliss of being in the realm of spirit, where there is no worry or guilt.

When you encounter a personal dilemma about what you want to go after in your life, turn the decision over to your sacred self: "Decide for me. I leave it in your hands." Then let go and listen. Your answers will come as you develop the internal willingness to allow your higher self to guide you. Miraculously, the right person will show up and say precisely what you need to hear, or you will be guided to the right source. To do this, you must let go and allow your higher awareness to exercise itself.

When you allow yourself to be still, you will understand the futility of constant striving and chasing after more.

Keep in mind the advice offered in *A Course in Miracles*: "Only infinite patience produces immediate results."

By giving yourself moments for appreciation, you allow yourself the freedom to arrive rather than strive. You choose to be free of ego demands and allow the loving presence to be felt.

Wayne Dyer is the author of nine books, including *Your Sacred Self* (HarperCollins)

47

Power in the Positive

by Norman Vincent Peale

Undoubtedly, there are people today who have within themselves astonishing power. I think that may be said of everyone, and yet we allow the smallest and most insignificant things to frustrate our power. I do not know what constitutes an obstacle in the way of your success or happiness. But I do know that it is not necessary for you to be hobbled, hampered, or defeated.

I am constantly amazed at the astonishing power that can be released in people by the simple habit of positive thinking, which is another term for faith. Anyone who becomes a great person did so because he or she refused to be a little person and refused to allow obstacles to defeat him or her. The most inspirational thing in life is a person who has overcome obstacles and hardships.

But, you may say, "I've tried positive thinking, and things didn't turn out right."

Who said everything would turn out right? And what do you mean by "right"? Do you mean as you wanted? How do you know that your idea, the thing you wanted, was in harmony with God's idea? It is my humble belief that when you and I are willing to put ourselves in harmony with God's ideas, not trying stubbornly to force our own way, then things turn out right. That does not necessarily mean as we thought we wanted.

Positive thinking is realistic thinking. It always sees the negative, but it doesn't dwell on the negative and nurture it, letting it dominate the mind. It keeps the negative in proper size and grows the positive big.

Those who are skeptical about positive thinking will cite instances where it didn't seem to get results. But what, or who, was at fault? Was it the principles of positive thinking? Or was it the person who was using it, or who thought he or she was?

"If you have faith," says the most reliable document ever written, "nothing shall be impossible." And how do you release it? You release it by changing the cast of your thoughts. By practicing belief rather than disbelief. You probably go along every day affirming, "I cannot do that, I cannot do this."

"I can't." How many times a day do you say, "I cannot do it"? All you have to do is repeat that negative thought to your subconscious mind and it will become a fact, because your subconscious mind wants to believe it anyway. Then you come up with a proposition and you hopefully ask your subconscious mind, "Can I, or can't I?" Your subconscious mind will answer that you cannot do it. You have trained it to answer negatively. Your creative imagination has formed a picture of yourself as failing. As you think, so are you. You have thought yourself into a state of disbelief in yourself.

If, over a long period of time, you create in your mind the picture that you cannot, you will inevitably have a picture of yourself failing and, therefore, you will fail. You have two powers within you, creative imagination and will. You may summon your will, which will say, "I can." But your creative imagination says, "No, you cannot." In this conflict of opinion, you cannot, because your creative imagination is stronger than your will. This is true because imagination is in the realm of belief, and what you believe in your heart determines what you can or cannot do.

If, over time, you believe that with the help of God you can overcome, you can achieve, then you will get a deep, unshakable, picture that you can. Then your will and your imagination flow together, and against that power nothing negative can stand.

Philosopher William James once said, "Believe, and your belief will in time create the fact." And Ralph Waldo Emerson said, "Beware of what you want, because there is a strong likelihood that you will get it." If you want some bad thing and keep forming a picture of it, you will get it. It will come to you. The whole universe will conspire to give it to you. If, on the contrary, you want some good thing, picture it, believe it, until it becomes your real desire: If you seek with all your heart, you shall find. Get into your mind positive convictions about what you want to be, what you want to become, and what you want to do. And you will go far toward attaining your goal.

If there is still in your mind the idea that you cannot do something, the reason you do not accomplish it is because you are thinking negatively. Start believing; start having faith. And presently, you will attain results. Identify yourself with success, and success will come to you.

The Bible points out that you have to repent and forgive if you want faith to operate in your life. You have to get all sin out. Did you commit a sin yesterday? And are you sorry for it? Then repent and ask for forgiveness, and don't let it linger in consciousness as guilt. If it does, it will burrow down into your unconscious and will block power in your life.

You can't get much faith through a person who is filled with sin, wrong, and guilt. To have a flow of this power through a personality, to release it, you must have a transformed personality. You have to get rid of hate, ill will, grudges, and sins, for they block power. Only a little power trickles through, not enough to give great strength.

So form in your mind a picture of yourself believing, achieving, what God wants you to do and to be. Cleanse yourself so that His power may get through you. No matter what obstacles are before you, if you will cleanse yourself and believe, you will obtain absolutely astonishing feats.

Throw back your shoulders, let your heart sing, let your eyes flash, let your mind be lifted up. Live with verve and victory and enthusiasm, such as you have never had before. Leave those old negative defeats at the altar of God. And like Joan of Arc, let Him touch your bright and shining sword and storm the walls of defeat to conquer them.

This excerpt was taken from *In God We Trust* by the late Norman Vincent Peale and is printed with permission from the Peale Center.

48

Giving and Receiving Criticism

by Patti Hathaway

Criticism is an indispensable part of our lives. If we can understand and use it, criticism can empower us to become better people. Why, then, do so many of us resist taking full advantage of what can be such an enormous benefit?

One reason why we tend to resist criticism is that a good part of our self-image is based on how others view us. When we find out that someone sees us in a less than positive light, we can feel devastated.

People tend to like to hear what is consistent with their own views and to resist ideas contrary to their belief structures. If we knew we were doing something ineffectively, wouldn't we automatically try to improve the deficiency? Criticism implies that we could be wrong. What could be more personal and threatening? It takes an open mind to be able to listen to an opposing view.

There are basically three types of criticism that we experience: 1) valid, or bona fide, criticism, 2) unjustified, or invalid criticism, and 3) criticism that is vague or is simply a difference of opinion.

As the recipient of criticism, we have more control than the critic, once the criticism has been delivered. It is then up to us to decide whether we believe the criticism has merit and is worth acting upon.

We experience three stages when coping with criticism: 1) Awareness—be aware that criticism is "just criticism" and then move quickly to assess its merit; 2) Assessment—assess how the criticism was delivered, the intention of the critic, and how valid you believe the criticism to be; and 3) Action—decide what action, if any, you want to take with the criticism.

Action Strategies

Let's examine some action strategies for dealing assertively with criticism.

1. Fogging. When faced with unjustified criticism, force yourself to avoid counter criticism or counter manipulating your critic. Instead, use the assertiveness skill called "fogging." This is simply calm acknowledgment of the possibility that there may be some truth in the criticism.

2. Admitting the truth. Admitting the truth is very effective when handling valid criticism. The first thing we must do when handling valid criticism is to accept it as valid, but not fall into exaggerated put-downs and negative self-talk. Avoid overapologizing or overcompensating for your error.

3. Requesting specific feedback. This sample response leads us into the third and probably most powerful technique you can use in handling valid criticism—requesting specific feedback. With the use of questions, you can begin focusing on the future instead of dwelling on the past. The act moves you directly into the *action* stage and forces the negative critic to look at potential solutions instead of belaboring your failure. Also, it enlists the critic to be on your side.

Guidelines for Giving Criticism

In giving criticism, let's first look at some positive results of criticism. Open criticism can relieve stress, permitting people to stop playing games of guessing at each other's expectations and evaluation of one another. Criticism can improve interpersonal relationships, for honesty promotes trust and paves the way to intimacy.

Criticism, correctly given, provides feedback that can improve job performance and promote continuing professional and personal development. Organizations that utilize criticism as a management tool enjoy higher levels of productivity and morale owing to their fostering a culture of openness. Openness is one of the components that can lead to excellence in organizations.

1. Set realistic goals and expectations. The first and most basic step we must take before we can give criticism is to let the other person know our expectations of him or her. If we have never shared our expectations, we have no basis on which to base our evaluation or criticism. A question every critic must ask himself or herself is, "Did I set up realistic expectations on which to base my evaluation?"

2. Be immediate. Once you have mutually agreed upon expectations, you need to observe the other person's behavior and be prepared to give positive or negative feedback, depending on the outcome of his or her actions. If someone has done a good job, don't just keep quiet: praise that person for it. Criticism can be positive as well as negative, and helpings of the former can help us tolerate doses of the latter. Give the feedback as close to the actual event as possible. Be short and specific. Select a good time, but don't save up your comments until you have a 15-minute litany to discharge. When giving criticism, you should not ask for a complete character change. It is far more effective to address one trait or issue at a time.

It is a good idea to be sensitive to timing when you are going to criticize another person. If he or she is already under a great deal of stress, you may elect to wait until he or she would be able to listen to you and do something about the criticism. You may want to put yourself in the other person's shoes and ask yourself how you would feel receiving the criticism at that time. Giving criticism requires compassion, insight, and tact.

3. Be specific. What we often omit in the formula is the action-oriented specify step. A part of us really wants an apology or some kind of guilt-ridden response from the other person after we tell him or her how we feel. One of the most important steps in giving criticism is to specify a corrective action. This allows the person criticized to do something about the criticism rather than just react defensively to our expression of negative feeling.

Giving and receiving criticism are difficult yet essential skills for each of us to master. By opening ourselves to criticism, we can learn how to improve ourselves both personally and professionally. If we are completely satisfied with where we're at and not willing to accept criticism, we probably will not proceed much further in our careers or experience much growth and satisfaction in our lives. Thomas Edison once said, "Show me a thoroughly satisfied man, and I will show you a failure."

Providing others with honest feedback in the form of criticism can deepen our interpersonal relationships with them and can provide us—and them—with the tools necessary to improve productivity and self-esteem.

Patti Hathawy is a speaker, trainer and corporate consultant. She is the author of *Giving and Receiving Criticism* from which this article is adapted.

49

Courage to Change

by Sheila Murray Bethel

Courage can take many forms. The challenges of daily life are often far more difficult than those offered by cataclysmic events.

Do you have the courage to be honest with yourself and to do and say what the following 10 items suggest?

1. The courage to seek the truth. I am willing to seek out unpleasant truths, even when they conflict with things I have invested in, or when the truth threatens my physical, intellectual, or emotional security. I recognize that my personal freedom depends on my ability to seek and find truth.

2. The courage to lead an ethical life. In a cynical world, I realize that it takes courage to be ethical. I resist the temptation to be less than ethical, even when "everyone is doing it." I regard honest people as heroes, not fools.

3. The courage to be involved. Apathy and indifference can be more devastating than any disaster. Despite occasional "compassion fatigue," I remain committed to making a difference and getting others involved. I refuse to look the other way.

4. The courage to reject cynicism. Cynicism is a comforting and protective refuge, but one I resist vigilantly. I know that trust and optimism, essential to a productive life, are impossible if I give in to the cowardice of cynicism.

5. The courage to assume responsibility. I alone am responsible for my actions, whether they lead to success or failure. I refuse to waste time on making excuses, harboring unrealistic hopes, or placing blame. I willingly share responsibility and accountability with others, and back them up 100 percent if things go wrong.

6. The courage to lead at home. I know that my home and family are my most powerful legacy for the future. I mentor my children, giving them equal love and discipline. I'm there 100 percent for my partner. I honor my parents and older relatives, even if advanced age, ill health, or different values make communication difficult and unrewarding. I live each day with my family and won't think, "Tomorrow I'll have more time."

7. The courage to persist. I have the courage to delay gratification, endure the long haul, and make sacrifices when necessary. I frequently visualize the next few years and anticipate the results of my actions. I summon the inner resources to stay on track by keeping my eye on this big picture.

8. The courage to serve. In an ego-driven, success-oriented society, I put myself second. I realize that the loftiest leader is the one who serves others best. My job, no matter what the description or title, is to provide satisfaction, solve problems, fill needs, and find answers in ways that enhance and empower those around me.

9. The courage to lead. Few people are willing to stand for something, or even to clarify what they would stand for if they could. Others criticize without offering solutions, but I concentrate on what I stand for, on solutions and goals, and on how I can motivate others to action. I'm not content to wait for someone else to take charge.

10. The courage to follow. Unlike leaders of image, a leader of substance knows when and how to follow willingly. I have learned the benefits of being a good follower, of welcoming the ideas and contributions of others without feeling that my position or integrity has been challenged.

A courageous leader is one who is willing to change, to grow, and to make a difference!

Sheila Murray Bethel, author of *Making a Difference,* is a speaker, consultant, and chair of the Bethel Leadership Institute in Burlingame, California.

50

The Power of Forgiveness

by John Gray

To *fully open* each other and enjoy a lifetime of love, we must learn the most important skill of all, forgiveness. Forgiving others for their mistakes not only frees you to love again but allows you to forgive yourself for not being perfect.

When we don't forgive in one relationship, our love is restricted in all our relationships. We can still love others, but not as much. When a heart is blocked in one relationship, it beats more weakly in them all. Forgiveness allows us to give our love again and helps us to open up both to give and also to receive love. When we are closed, we lose on two counts.

The more you love someone, the more you suffer when you don't forgive them. Many people are driven to suicide by the agonizing pain of not forgiving a loved one. The greatest pain we can ever feel is the pain of not forgiving someone we love.

This agony drives people mad and is responsible for all the violence and craziness in our world and in our relationships. It is this pain of holding back our love that moves many people to addictive behaviors, substance abuse, and random violence.

We stubbornly hold on to bitterness and resentment not because we are not loving, but because we do not know how to forgive. If we were not loving, then ceasing to love someone would not be painful at all. The more loving we are, the more painful it is to not forgive.

How We Learn to Forgive

If when we were children our parents had asked for our forgiveness when they made mistakes, we would know how to forgive. If we had watched them forgive each other, we would better know how to forgive. If we had experienced being forgiven for our own mistakes, we would not only know how to forgive but would have experienced firsthand the power of forgiveness to transform others. Because our parents did not know how to forgive, we easily misunderstand what it means. Emotionally, we associate forgiving someone with the realization that what they did was not so bad after all.

For example, let's say that I am late and you are upset with me. If I give you a great reason or excuse, you are more inclined to forgive me. Let's say I tell you, for instance, that my car blew up on the way over. That's why I am late. Surely, you would be more inclined to forgive me. Better yet, let's say a car blew up next to me and I stopped to save a child from dying. With such a "good" reason for being late, I would immediately be forgiven. But real forgiveness is needed when something really bad or hurtful happens and there is no good reason for it.

Real forgiveness acknowledges that a real mistake has been made and then affirms that the person who made it still deserves to be loved and respected. It does not mean that you condone or agree with their behavior in any way. You acknowledge that a mistake was made that you want corrected or at least not repeated.

When forgiveness is learned and expressed, a huge weight is lifted. Through saying those three simple words, "I forgive you," lives and relationships have been dramatically saved again and again.

Practicing Forgiving

The power to forgive is within us all, but like any other skill we must practice it. In the beginning, it takes time. We work at forgiving our partner, and then suddenly, the next day we are blaming them again. This is par for the course. Mastering the advanced relationship skill of forgiveness takes time, but with practice, it becomes a natural response.

In the beginning, a helpful phrase you can write out or think is: "Nobody's perfect, so I forgive you for being imperfect. What you did was wrong. Nobody deserves to be treated the way you treated me. What you did was wrong and I forgive you. I forgive you for not being perfect. I forgive you for not giving me the love and respect that I deserve. I forgive you for not knowing better. I wish for you the decency and respect that every human being deserves. I forgive you for making a mistake."

Christ's message to humanity from the cross was one of forgiveness. To rise above death, beyond pain, one has to forgive. His words were: "Father, forgive them; for they know not what they do." In this simple phrase is contained the secret of how to forgive.

We can begin to forgive our partners and others who hurt us when we can recognize that they really don't know what they are doing.

I remember when I first experienced pure forgiveness. It was when my daughter Lauren was two years old. She was playing with her food. I kept telling her not to, but she went ahead anyway. Within a few moments she was holding the spaghetti in her hands, then dropping it all over our carpet.

I was furious inside because she had made a mess and I had to clean it up. At the same time, however, I was completely forgiving of her. I was angry with her, but my heart was completely open and filled with love.

I wondered how this could be and then remembered Christ's words, "Father, forgive them; for they know not what they do."

In that moment it was easy to forgive her because she clearly didn't know what she was doing when she dropped the spaghetti. I suppose she thought she was creating a work of art! What she didn't realize was that she was causing a problem for me.

Why People Don't Forgive

As a counselor I have repeatedly experienced that people act and react in nonloving ways when they don't know better. People bear grudges out of ignorance and innocence. When they can experience a better way, they go for it. No one in their heart of hearts really wants to withhold and punish. It is merely the only way he or she knows to react when another person disrespects them.

We have problems because "we know not what we do." Once we bear this truth in mind and heart, our mistakes and our partners' mistakes are more forgivable.

The angels in heaven rejoice each time you forgive. When you choose to love instead of closing your heart, you bring a little spark of divinity into our dark world of struggle. You lighten the load of others and help them to forgive as well.

When men and women fail in relationships, it is not because they are not loving. We are all born with love in our hearts and a purpose to fulfill. We experience pain in our relationships because we do not know how to share our love in ways that work.

We are missing the skills.

Making a Difference

Through practicing forgiveness, we are not only creating a lifetime of love for ourselves, but we are making a difference in the world.

Imagine a world where families are not shattered by divorce or neighbors are not hating each other. This kind of world is possible. Each step you take in your relationship helps actualize that possibility.

It is naive to assume that we can create peace in the world when we cannot make peace with the people we love. When our leaders are capable of having loving and mutually nurturing family relationships, then they will have acquired the skills to negotiate world peace.

Each time we take the sometimes painful or difficult step to positive resolution in our personal relationships, we are paving the way for harmony in the world. Your every effort and attempt make it easier for others to follow you. If you cannot make forgiveness work, what hope is there for others? But if you can, who among us cannot succeed? May you and your loved ones experience a lifetime of love, and in our lives may we also share the experience of a world filled with love.

John Gray is the best-selling author of many books, including *What Your Mother Coundln't Tell You & What Your Father Didn't Know.*

51

Everybody's Doing It? That's No Excuse!

by Laura Schlessinger

Every day on my radio program I talk with people who have gotten themselves into all sorts of troubled, unhappy and unworkable situations because they put aside questions of what was sensible, good, right, legal, moral, or holy, and turned instead to what they thought were worthy, viable alternatives.

And always, they have excuses—excuses that may sound good but that don't stand up to careful examination.

"This is the 1990s, you know. Things are different now," people say to me. But I wonder which came first—the 1990s or the "things"? The fault lies not in our decade but in ourselves.

"But everyone is doing it—it's no big deal," is another slogan I often hear.

I am struck by how scary that concept can be. Groups, crowds and mobs are not often known for moral or responsible behavior. In fact, there are plenty of studies suggesting that large groups can do things that the people involved would be ashamed to do on an individual basis.

In the final analysis, the "everybody's doing it" excuse amounts to dropping humanity to its lowest common denominator.

"But I thought it would work out—I thought we were different," I'm told.

It's amazing how strongly we want to think that common sense and moral values are for the stupid, weak, uninspired, mundane "others." Clearly they aren't for us because we are special, exempt from the flaws of others in some magical way.

It's sad that we don't appreciate the commonality of our desires, needs, passions, excitement, thrills, infatuations and temptations. However unique they feel to us, our feelings are actually much like other people's and are no excuse to evade moral responsibility.

Do people really believe that the negative consequences of their actions are neutralized because of their own uniqueness? Do they really think that their motivations must be acceptable simply because they come from "strong feelings"?

We should see such feelings as challenges, opportunities to acknowledge our human weaknesses and rise above them.

Recently I talked with a young woman who has lately been exploring her own spirituality. She asked my opinion about ritual of selfdenial such as the Christian period of Lent, in which people give up something they desire for a brief period of time.

"Isn't this just an empty ritual?" she wondered.

I think not. As a practicing conservative Jew, I compare the self-denial of Lent to the Jewish High Holy Days, which are occasions of fasting, and to the Kashrut, or Kosher Laws. Like Lent, these customs provide the inspiration to rise to the challenge of a holy commandment. The also provide a useful experience of self-discipline and sacrifice.

The act of sacrifice, even a symbolic sacrifice for a brief time, can help us realize how our everyday life lacks a focus on the deeper meaning and motivation of our life, and how focused we usually are on stimulation, acquisition and ego-gratification. Intentionally making ourselves uncomfortable through such holy rituals can be enlightening, teaching us something about our hidden weaknesses and potential strengths.

In truth the interplay between such weakness and strengths guides our personal decisions, not the ambience of the decade of the example of a faceless "everybody."

Sadly, we often come to this realization only after our actions have undermined our lives.

Dr. Laura Schlessinger is the author of *How Could You Do That?* and host of her own radio program.

52

The Emancipation Proclamation

by Ken Shelton

Once on a trip to the island of Jamaica in the Caribbean, I found myself waiting for a ride back to the hotel after playing a round of golf. I then met four bus and taxi drivers who were waiting there for other people to finish their rounds. We struck up a conversation.

I sensed from three of the men a high degree of resignation with their current status. They felt that they were just one step removed from the old sugar plantations, driving busses for owners who paid them low wages and would never cut them in on the action.

But the fourth man was different. He owned his own car (a 10-year-old Chevrolet in immaculate condition) and had his own taxi business. He had been driving the roads of Jamaica for many years, and seemed to know half the people on the island. If they didn't know him personally, they at least knew his car. After listening to his colleagues gripe and moan about their "hopeless" condition, he spoke to them: "You never want to give in and give up," he said. "If you have faith and work toward the modest goal of owning your own car, you can do it. This is no miracle. I did it. You can do it. We are not slaves. We are free men, and we—you and I—can own and manage our own business."

He said this emphatically, in a deep, "James Earl Jones" voice. It was as if God Himself had spoken. Even so, the other three men were so deeply resigned to their fate that they were more amused than motivated by his remarks. With their minds on the plantation, they couldn't imagine a new freedom and identity.

Now What?

Elephant trainers say that once a young elephant accepts the limitations imposed by a heavy chain on its leg, it will not try to break away later even when the chain is replaced with a light rope. In its mind, it is still in captivity or, at least, confinement.

Many people, too, are reluctant to leave the "plantation"— a demeaning job, a fraudulent company, a confining condition, an abusive relationship, a violent neighborhood—even when their "chains" (physical, emotional, social, or legal restraints) are removed. At least, there on the plantation, they have some measure of security and identity.

Modern plantations still seem to work, at least as money-making units, because people at least have a sense of place—a roof, a role, a routine, a goal, and even some reward for good behavior. Of course, even convicted criminals have all that. But mental ruts and physical routines are as good as prison bars and gates. No need for chains when habits will do.

Once you leave the planation, you may not know what to do. You're on your own. You may be good, but good for what? When your whole life has been spent in servitude on a plantation—taking orders, responding to crises, doing a simple repetitive task—you naturally feel a bit unsettled when you gain newfound freedom or identity.

A new identity, or true identity, is often the first fruit coming from a personal "roots" experience. That's when you learn that you are not your job; you are not your present condition; you are not your past experience. Nor do you need to be a victim of your conditions and conditioning. You see that your roots sink deep into human history and family genealogy and connect with divine creation. It often takes true self-identity to preserve, protect, and expand personal freedoms.

Emancipation, then, is the first step toward authentic personal leadership—emancipation not only from the plantation-like organizations of our lives, but also from your own self-made cells and self-defeating behaviors.

I place heavy emphasis on starting with self. Otherwise, once off one plantation, you will likely just join another. To "make ends meet," some people will justify any and all means. But a repeated pattern of "rational lies" makes a sad life story.

Write Your Own Emancipation Proclamation and Plan

If you feel a need to be free of someone or something in your life, I invite you to write your own emancipation proclamation. In writing your proclamation, consider the following four steps.

1. Ask: From what (or whom) do I wish to be liberated? Think of your own bad habits and self-defeating behaviors first; otherwise, you will likely think that the whole problem is "out there" with other people and things. And with that attitude, you will likely either fight or flee to escape personal responsibility for results.

2. Write a first-person statement of liberation: I, (your name), proclaim myself to be free from illicit, unfair, unwise, secretive, possessive, and abusive relationships, including those in my private and professional life.

3. Create your liberation plan. How will you liberate yourself, and possibly other people? Consider these questions: What opposition will I face? How will I overcome it? Who might assist me (allies)? What resources can I gather and rally? How, when, and where will I start the campaign? How will I see it through to a successful conclusion?

4. Imagine yourself going through these steps. See yourself in a new condition, a new environment of your own choosing and making.

Abolishing plantation management in our time will cap the tremendous gains in civil and human rights made by pioneers and martyrs in many countries in recent decades and days. Only then can people sing, as did Martin Luther King, Jr., "Free at last, free at last. God Almighty, we are free at last."

Ken Shelton is chairman and editor in chief of Executive Excellence Publishing and the author of *Beyond Counterfeit Leadership: How You Can Become a More Authentic Leader.*

ABOUT THE EDITOR

Ken Shelton is chairman and editor-in-chief of Executive Excellence Publishing, publishers of newsletters, magazines, books, audio books, and CD-ROMs on personal and organizational development. The mission of Executive Excellence Publishing is to "help you find a wiser, better way to live your life and lead your organization."

Since 1984, Ken has served as editor of *Executive Excellence,* the world's leading executive advisory newsletter, and more recently *Personal Excellence,* a digest of the best thinking on personal and professional development. He is the editor of several books, including *In Search of Quality,* and *A New Paradigm of Leadership,* and the author of *Beyond Counterfeit Leadership: How You Can Become a More Authentic Leader.*

For many years, he has enjoyed a close association with Stephen R. Covey, primarily as a writer and editor on various projects, including *The 7 Habits of Highly Effective People, Principle-Centered Leadership,* and *First Things First.* He is a former editor of *Utah Business* and *BYU Today* and a contributing writer to several other magazines.

Ken has a master's degree in mass and organizational communications from Brigham Young University and San Diego State University. In San Diego, California, he worked four years as a marketing communications specialist for General Dynamics Aerospace. He now lives in Provo, Utah, with his wife, Pam, and their three sons.

The Best of Personal Excellence represents but a sample of the meaningful material to be found in every issue of *Personal Excellence* magazine.

Executive Excellence

Since 1984, *Executive Excellence* has provided business leaders and managers with the best and latest thinking on leadership development, managerial effectiveness, and organizational productivity. Each issue is filled with insights and answers from top business executives, trainers, and consultants—information you won't find in any other publication.

CONTRIBUTING EDITORS INCLUDE

"Excellent! This is one of the finest newsletters I've seen in the field."

—Tom Peters, co-author of *In Search of Excellence*

"Executive Excellence is the Harvard Business Review *in* USA Today *format."*

—Stephen R. Covey, author of *The 7 Habits of Highly Effective People*

"Executive Excellence is the best executive advisory newsletter anywhere in the world—it's just a matter of time before a lot more people find that out."

—Ken Blanchard, co-author of *The One-Minute Manager*

Stephen R. Covey

Ken Blanchard

Marjorie Blanchard

Charles Garfield

Peter Senge

Gifford Pinchot

Elizabeth Pinchot

Warren Bennis

Brian Tracy

For more information about *Executive Excellence* or *Personal Excellence*, or for information regarding books, audio tapes, CD-ROMs, custom editions, reprints, and other products, please call Executive Excellence Publishing at:

1-800-304-9782
or visit our web site: **http://www.eep.com**